trotman

Multiple Job Offers in 10 Days

Your two-week plan to
finding a great job

Jonathan R. Price

Multiple Job Offers in 10 Days

First published in the United States by Careers Press, Inc, in 2004.
First published in Great Britain in 2009 by Trotman Publishing, an
imprint of Crimson Publishing, Westminster House, Kew Road,
Richmond, Surrey TW9 2ND

Copyright © 2007, 2009 by Chokoloskee Ventures, LLC

Author Jonathan R. Price

British Library Cataloguing in Publication Data
A catalogue record for this book is available from the British Library

ISBN: 978 1 84455 214 6

Typeset by Cambridge Publishing Management Ltd
Printed and bound in the UK by MPG Books Ltd, Bodmin

Contents

About the Author   v

Acknowledgements   vii

Foreword   ix

Introduction: What This Book Isn't – And What It Is   1

1. Day 1: Understanding Your Marketability   9

2. Day 2: The CV and Covering Letter   15

3. Day 3: Who to Get in Front of and How   31

4. Days 4 and 5: Getting Your CV Out There . . .   45

5. Day 6: What to Expect, What Not to Expect, and Why   55

6. Days 7–9: How to Handle the Interviews   75

7. Day 10: Accepting Several Job Offers!   87

8. Negotiating the Best Possible Salary   95

9. Your Ongoing Job Search (aka Your Second Career)   109

10. Your Marketing Approach: You Don't Have One!   117

11. Your Career Choices: Why Are You Looking For Work?   129

12. The Scary Truth About the 'Holy Trinity'!   133

13. Why You Are Unemployed or Still in the Same Old Job   149

14. The Fears, Phobias and Fallacies Holding You
Back (And How to Overcome Them)   159

Conclusion   163

Further Information   165

Index   167

About the Author

Jonathan R. Price is the senior manager for one of the leading executive career advancement firms in the USA. Jonathan has used these same proven methods to help his clients land jobs earning £30,000, £100,000, £300,000, and even more! He has an education and professional background in medicine, education and business. He lives and works in sunny Fort Myers, Florida.

Check him out on the Web at www.multiple-job-offers.com

Acknowledgements

There are several people who are near and dear to me that made this book not only possible, but are the real reason it was written. These are the people whom I work with on a daily basis, they are my colleagues, they are my friends and, in my mind, they are my family. Words can't express just how much they have helped, but I'll give it a try anyway.

Nancy Eardley – Proposal proofreading. Chapter proofreading. Nancy was my first line editor. Thanks to her I didn't look like a totally inept moron to my editors at the publishing house. (Luckily Nancy already knows how bad my writing is and she graciously agreed to make me look good. Big thanks to her!) Nancy has really been my cheerleader and my coach throughout the book. She kept me on track when I veered off into the lazy life, and she kept me excited even when it meant that I ate at my desk every day for six weeks during the final push. I feel that she has written this book just as much as I have.

Kim Clower – Proposal proofreading. Various research projects. Formatting of CVs, and help with the mail merge tutorial. She has also given me advice, support and inspiration. She is one of my best friends and I am always glad she is there to talk about the book – and all the other crazy things we discuss!

Gina Panettieri – My Agent. Wow – found a brand-new writer and immediately put me on the map. She was great, and took my writing virginity with laughter and enthusiasm.

Career Press/New Page Books – A great publishing company, with an all-star lineup of talented writers. I am incredibly grateful for the chance they took with me, and I can only hope that I live up to their expectations.

Michael W. Dean – *$30 Writing School* convinced me to get off the sofa and write a book!

George Devore – For great technical contributions and an in-depth understanding of puns.

Bruce and Nanette Scoville – For supporting me in this project, even though I am giving away all of their secrets, for mentoring me, for the genuine friendship they have provided, and for basically adopting me as their own. Bruce and Nanette taught me virtually everything I know about looking for work. Much of what is written in this book are the hard-learned tips, techniques and principles that they have developed throughout their years working with countless numbers of executives and professionals, listening to blowhard job-seekers tell these two well-meaning people that they are wrong, are only trying to take advantage of them, and are a scam; when in reality they were just telling a truth that most people can't stand to accept. Overcoming the status quo and convincing a person to finally try something different is a harder battle than most people realize.

You guys are terrific and I owe so much of what I have to your support and friendship.

Foreword

This book is a compendium of the knowledge that has been collected by myself, as well as the author, over the last decade of hard work. It has been the goal of our company and its staff, who have collaborated to make it as successful as it is today, to help people. That's what we do. When individuals find themselves cast adrift in the tumultuous sea of unemployment, it has been the job of highly gifted and caring people such as Jonathan to throw them a much-needed safety line, to pull them back in, and to provide them the succour and support that they so desperately need.

Helping people to find work is a tough job. Anyone who has had to find a new job knows that it can be a harder full-time job than anything else they've done in their career. In the 10-plus years that Jonathan has been with our firm, he has been instrumental in evolving not only a successful business, but also in developing approaches and strategies that help our clients land jobs, land them faster, and find opportunities that are better than they had hoped for.

Streamlining the CV-creation process is one of the most critical improvements we've had in our business. When I first launched my company, creating a CV was a long, arduous task that involved dozens of hours of labour on the part of a professional writer, with several weeks of painful and time-consuming back and forth sessions between the client and the writer, trying to boil down dozens of years of work history into a document that made sense and still conveyed to the reader who our client was, and what he or she had to offer.

Today, our clients not only have a new CV within a couple of days of coming on board, they also have learned how to create a CV! The process that Jonathan pioneered has led to our clients receiving better responses to the mailings, having better interviews, and reporting that they are better able to communicate their strengths and successes in the interview and evaluation process.

In this book, Jonathan has given away the store. He has shared with you, the reader, all of the hard-earned secrets and lessons that we've learned the 'hard way'. That's OK. That's why we're here – to help people. Good luck with your job search.

Bruce B. Scoville
Founder and CEO, Barton Industries Inc.

Introduction

What This Book Isn't – And What It Is

First, let me explain what this book *isn't*. It isn't a dry, theoretical, non-fiction book. I don't like non-fiction. I refused to buy textbooks when I was at university. (I took good notes and really listened to the lecturers instead.) This is also not a book written by a professional writer who has done some research on finding jobs and is trying to think back to the last time he had to look for real work.

This isn't about theories. Just cold hard facts and proven methods. Methods proven by me and by thousands of my clients. My clients have used them to generate multiple offers – and made the most of those opportunities. Now that's out of the way, let me explain who I am and what this book is.

My name is Jonathan Price. I'm not a recruitment consultant or a career coach. I don't contact companies to see if they have a job vacancy to be filled, and I don't give people personality tests to analyse what makes them happy. The best way to describe what I do is to say I am an Executive Career Marketer. Over the last decade I have provided marketing to thousands of professionals, helping them find their next job in the fastest way I know how. I've worked with entry-level employees, recent graduates (even secondary school students) all the way to chief executives.

This book is about teaching you how to do for yourself exactly what I have done for my clients: get the exposure you need to find your next great job. You've probably heard of the 'Hidden Job Market'. Well, that approach is the wrong way round. The only thing hidden in the job market is YOU! In preparing to write this book, I read most of the other books on this subject. Some of them were OK, a couple were even quite good, but a few weren't great. Quality aside, none of those books told me how to actually generate significant activity in my job search. Let's face it: that's really what's important – and that's what this book *is* going to show you how to do.

I'll be honest. The main reason none of the other books you looked at told you how to get real results in creating multiple job offers is because the authors don't know how to. The authors have researched the subject, but they've never actually done it.

'Looking for work effectively is a full-time occupation.'

The company I work for shares the same basic information that is in this book with our prospective clients, and some of them actually take that knowledge away with them and DO IT. A significant number of those people realise that this is more work than they are willing to do, and they pay my company to do it for them. It's worth it, and nine out of ten times clients see that value almost immediately. In this book I will share all my experience, knowledge, and 'secrets' with you. Then I will encourage you to go out there and DO IT. Because in my experience, this is the most effective strategy for finding a great job.

How Do I Know This Is The Best Way To Find Work?

If you have ever looked for a job, it's very likely that you have been given advice on how to go about it. Probably from your family, your friends, maybe even a trusted mentor. They all had your best interests in mind, but their advice is probably the worst thing you'll ever receive! Why?

Answer this simple question: does your friend, or family member, or mentor look for work on a full-time basis? The answer is no. They do not look for work every day. They might look at CVs occasionally as part their work. They might even interview potential employees for their companies, but they aren't out there looking for work. Put simply, they have no idea about how to find a job effectively and quickly. Think of going to them for advice on looking for work as going to your Great Aunt Mabel (who makes the best apple crumble in the whole family) and asking her if you should go with the single or quadruple bypass surgery. It may sound funny, but it could have as serious an impact on your life.

I can't tell you how many times I have spoken to successful, intelligent people who have had a great career, earning upwards of

£65,000 a year for a decade or more – up to a year ago. Now they're working at a DIY store making £5.79 an hour, wondering if 49 is too early to retire and how to make ends meet.

How did they end up there? Was it alcohol, drugs, or gambling? No. It was the well-meant advice from their friends. I don't want to scare you. But I have to. It's not a joke, and you can't imagine how fast things spiral out of control when you don't have a solid, proven plan in place to find work quickly. But there is light at the end of this depressing tunnel I'm leading you down. I have seen that same individual literally take off the shop apron, pack a bag, and go off to another city to interview for a management job with a company almost as big as the one he or she was just working in as a Customer Advisor. (And get that job.) I've worked with clients who have overcome much bigger obstacles than that.

Before you put this book down, thinking that this is just for executives, or that this is the same as those adverts with the disclaimer 'These results are unique and will never happen for you', let me reassure you: this is a perfect match for you.

The approach you will learn in this book is incredibly effective. (I'll let the cat out of the bag: we're going to be discussing direct marketing. Don't be scared; it's not a dirty word, nor is it difficult.) The best part about it is that it works at every level of your career.

How Do I Know This Approach Will Work For You?

I showed a young woman called Jennifer, fresh out of university, with a business degree, how to conduct a direct marketing campaign to find her first job. We worked together for two days sorting out the mess her university tutor had made of her CV. Then we identified the top 100 companies in her area. They were all companies where she could apply her new degree and offer value to the employer. We directed her CV and covering letter, by name and title, to the appropriate person in each of those companies, the 'recruiting decision-maker'. (You'll be learning a lot more about these people later on.) A few days after her letters went out in the post, Jennifer called me, completely in a panic. She had been getting several calls a day and had scheduled three and four interviews a day, for the next four days. She didn't know what to do. I calmed her down. (Can you imagine how exciting it would be to go through a similar experience?) I explained to her that she was to go to each of those interviews, give her best effort using the strategies that we had discussed previously, and, if they offered her the job, accept it. Every single one of them. The following week Jennifer called me, again in a panic. She had just finished her interviews and she had officially accepted EIGHT JOBS!

Of course she didn't start all eight of those jobs. Before you think that what Jennifer did was wrong, be aware that your next potential employer is playing the same game with you, time and time again. (Ever gone to an interview where they tell you that they think you fit the bill, but so-and-so is on holiday, or HR has to send some paperwork to you? You'll soon learn that what actually happened was that you were the runner-up, they'd already offered the job to someone else, and they were keeping you in reserve in case the other person didn't accept the job.) Jennifer and I laid all these opportunities out on the table, and reviewed each of them. Jennifer chose the best three offers, based on initial pay and, more importantly, the career path available to her. We then worked together to maximise her opportunities, negotiating a higher starting salary with the company that she most wanted to work for. They agreed, and today she is still at that company, only now she's two grades higher. Just a year out of university and she is now an assistant director in one of the largest companies in her town! Trust me. This approach works. It works every day for my clients and I know it will work for you too.

How To Turn The Pitfalls Into Triumphs Using This Book!

I recently conducted a campaign for Gary, a professional in the manufacturing industry who secured a factory manager job, earning a little more than £45,000 a year, less than three weeks from the time we met – and that includes the time for Gary to decide to use my service; to help him create his marketing documents (his CV and covering letter); identify the companies that would be the best match for him; print, assemble, and deliver the envelopes to his doorstep (he lived across the country from me); get the envelopes in the post; answer the phone calls; schedule the interviews; negotiate the salary and accept the job!

Besides being the longest sentence you'll ever read, the preceding paragraph just summed up the entire process, from start to finish in three weeks. How easy was that?

If, after reading this far along in the book, you are sold on the idea that this is a great way to find a new job and you're ready to read ahead to the next chapters (the ones that really get into the meat of the matter), please do! You won't hurt my feelings if you stop reading my sales pitch and start using my knowledge. But, if you are still sceptical, I would like to propose something to you. I propose that I can guess *exactly* what you have been doing so far to find your next job. Also, I bet I can tell you *exactly* what the results have been so far. I bet that since you started looking for work (and I don't care if you're looking because you were laid off, moved to a new town, or just want to find something better than what you have now), you'll have been using what I describe as the 'Holy Trinity' of the job search.

Your job search probably started one of two ways: Either you started getting more and more disenchanted with your current job and slowly began toying with the idea of looking for something else, or you walked into work one day and your manager pulled you into his or her office and explained that the market had changed, the accountants had looked at the bottom line and, he hated to do it, but he had to let you go.

The first thing you did was dust off your old CV, add your most recent job, and start looking for places to send it to. Your first thought was the newspaper job vacancies and online job boards. So, you sent off for an application form for the jobs advertised in the paper and posted your CV in response to online vacancies. Some hard work, but fairly straightforward. Then, you sat back for a couple of weeks and waited for the calls to come in. Nothing? Or not much interest?

That's OK. You still have your network, plus, you've talked to several recruitment consultants who said they have some great opportunities that they will get back to you about soon. So, while you're waiting for that, you start calling all your contacts at other companies, your friends, your ex-colleagues, and the people in the groups you go to. They don't have anything concrete for you, but they will ask around and see what they find.

Great, the job search is in full gear now! You go back to the job ads in the local paper every week, you check your emails, you follow up on every nibble that comes your way, and you call your network again. You call the recruitment agencies you're working with.

Things are happening! It's now four weeks into your job search and you can feel the activity. You call your network, *again*. You make follow-up calls to the recruiters you're waiting to hear back from about those interviews they said they were going to send you on – just a couple more days, they tell you. You call your network, again. (How many of them are still taking your calls?)

It's now a little more than a month and a half into your job search, and you've been to a couple of interviews. One said you were 'overqualified' (that's code for 'you want too much money') and another interviewer said you looked like a good match, and he promised to get back to you in a week or so, to schedule a second interview. Things are really happening! Then it's eight weeks and nine and 10. The same scenario is playing out, like a broken record, over and over again. At first it all looked so good, so promising, so, so, hopeful. But not so much now . . . But the key to success is perseverance . . . isn't it? Or is it the definition of insanity – doing the same thing over and over again, but expecting different results? If any of this rings a bell, you need to keep reading.

'You don't know you're doing something wrong until someone tells you.'

I talk to lots of people every day about their job search (sometimes as many as 50), and I know how hard it can be – at least when you're doing it wrong. Good news: that will not be the case for you any longer!

Don't get me wrong. Conducting a job search is work. It's not a part time activity, not unless you already have a job and you're only doing this because you'd like to see if there's something better out there. (If that's the case, be prepared to find a lot of better things out there!)

The first week will *really* feel like work, but then you will be so busy – and so excited – going to interviews and accepting multiple job offers that you won't even realise how hard you're working. This may still sound unrealistic right now, but that's just because of the response you've been getting so far. It's all in the approach. The reality is you've been doing it wrong all along and no one has told you until now.

This book will change your life. I know it will, because I help my clients change their lives every day. This is the last piece of sales pitch you'll get from me. From now on, you and I are working together, and two of the things my friends and clients know about me are that I don't mince words and I don't hold anything back. I'm going to tell you some stuff that may hurt your feelings or burst some bubbles for you as we go along, but I'm only doing it because it's time someone told you.

The 10-Day Method

To make the job search easier to manage, I've broken down the whole process into 10 easy sections, each with a whole day to get it done. In Chapter 1 you'll be getting going, and by Chapter 7 you'll be well on your way! Let's get started.

1. Day 1

Understanding Your Marketability

One of the most important things for you to understand when you start your job search is what your transferable skills are. You have skills that are applicable to other jobs in other industries, regardless of where you are on the job ladder. Of course, the further along you are in your career, the more skills you have acquired, so there are more places you would fit. Ironically, for most people, the further along in their career they get, the more convinced they become that there *isn't* any other place where they could apply their skills. They aren't right; that's just what they think.

As you progress in your career, your skills become less and less task-specific and become more situation-orientated. What does that mean? Here's an example that will help clarify the point:

Gary started his career in manufacturing. His first job, while still at school, was at the local widget manufacturer. He started on the plant floor cleaning the equipment that made the sub-assemblies. Gary went off to university and studied engineering. When he graduated, he came back to his home town and went back to work for the widget plant, only this time as a Junior Engineer. Gary worked his way up the ladder for the next 18 years, eventually ending up as Senior Project Manager.

Times changed and, as it all too often does, the economy turned and widget-making moved overseas. Gary was made redundant. For the next six months Gary looked every day for another job as a project manager for another widget manufacturer, with no luck. The widgets were all being produced on another continent and Gary was obsolete. If Gary hadn't come to me, he would probably be a Customer Advisor in a DIY superstore for the rest of his 'career'. Why? Was Gary really obsolete? Absolutely not. He just couldn't/wouldn't look anywhere but straight down the path he had been following his whole career. He was a race horse with blinkers on: nothing could distract him from the finish line – but then they took the finish line away.

The critical thing that Gary overlooked was that he wasn't an entry level employee, working on the factory floor assembling widgets anymore. Gary was a manager. He directed people, kept budgets under control, and coordinated work and time lines and all sorts of things that really had nothing specifically to do with widgets. Those skills were completely transferable. Other types of manufacturers could benefit from those skills, as well as engineering firms, consulting practices, building contractors and . . .

When you stop making widgets and start managing people, it's really the same set of skills no matter where you work. The trick is to work out first what your transferable skills are. (What skills have you got that could be applied to other fields and different roles?) Then to demonstrate to the reader that those skills are transferable. (The reader is the recruiting manager at the appropriate level for the job you are looking for. You'll learn more about this person as we go along, but keep this in mind for now: EVERYTHING you do, you do with the reader in mind.)

Once Gary got his head around the idea that he didn't have to look for a job in a widget plant, we were able to start talking about what industry-specific skills he had. What were other types of manufacturing operations similar to widget-making? What were the things he enjoyed most about his last job? His favourite thing about his last job was that they moved him from one plant to another, so that he could reorganise their facilities. Gary was what we call a 'change manager' and he didn't even know it!

In the six months before I met Gary, he had sent his CV to 32 widget manufacturers around the country and about 10 other manufacturers that produced a subset of widgets. In that time, he had two telephone interviews, and that was it. After he and I discussed his options, we began targeting other types of manufacturers, consulting firms and engineering companies. We identified 498 companies in his first choice of locations that he and I agreed would be a good match for him. We both knew that if they had a need, he had the skills and abilities to bring value to those companies. While we were doing the work on the list, Gary and I were also working on his new CV and covering letter. He was making pretty much almost all the mistakes we'll be discussing later in the book, which is no surprise, because virtually everyone makes at least half of those mistakes on their CV! We beat his CV and covering letter into shape and then posted them to all the companies on his list.

That's right, Gary posted his CV to 498 companies that were a great match for him. Before we met, he could only find 42. Did I have a better list? Yes and no. I did have access to a great list, several in fact, but if I gave Gary access to those lists, I know Gary wouldn't have found more than a dozen additional companies. The problem wasn't access; the problem was understanding.

> 'When you take off the blinkers, the world
> opens up to you.'

Gary's manufacturing revelation isn't the only example out there, and being a manager or executive isn't a prerequisite to having transferable skills. Jennifer, the young woman straight out of university, had transferable skills. (How – when she hadn't even started her career yet?) Jennifer was on the student newspaper team at school, and she had a part-time job in the university's graphic arts department. She enjoyed journalism and writing. One of the companies she approached was the largest newspaper in her town. It was also the fifth-largest employer in town. Her business degree went a long way in getting her noticed, but her manager, the person she sent her CV to originally, was impressed with her background in journalism and felt that she would have a real aptitude for the role.

Her first job for the paper was as Assistant Circulation Manager. She didn't get the job because of her education, but because her past experience on a school newspaper had more impact than the degree. That is a transferable skill, and it belonged to a 20-year-old woman with no full-time experience!

✓ Your Day 1 Assignment

Step 1

■ Make a list of all the responsibilities you have had so far in your career.

- Make a separate list of every achievement you've had in your career.
- Make a third list of every challenge you've had to overcome in your career.

Take those three lists and review them. If there is any reference to a specific product, service, or industry, cross out those words – NOT the item, just the reference to what it was for or in. Once you've done that, sit back and think to yourself: do any of these things have a place in another company besides my previous employers? For each one of the items on your lists that you can answer yes to, put a tick next to it. When you have finished, you should have quite a surprising list of things. Why surprising? Because these are your transferable skills!

Step 2

Now that you have identified these transferable skills, the next step is to clearly define them. It is important that you are able to clearly define those skills yourself, otherwise you will never be able to communicate them effectively to anyone else.

On a new sheet of paper (or a new document on your computer) list each of the items that had a tick beside it. Be sure to leave at least two lines under each one. Once you've done that, go through the list, writing out exactly what that skill or responsibility involved and how you could use it in another field or job. Don't worry about being completely sure that you could use that skill or experience in another industry; what you're really doing here is stretching your brain. It's probably been a long time since your grey matter had such a workout. Believe me, it would much rather finish its rest than hurt itself forging new paths into the darkness.

Once you've gone through the list, read it back to yourself. Do you see a common theme running through it? Are you starting to see some new places that you could/should be focusing your attention out there in the job universe? If you are, great! If you're not, don't worry. Some people's brains just fight harder against change. If you already have started thinking of other jobs and industries, jot them down straight away. Don't let those little gems get away. (In 10 minutes you might forget them or, worse yet, you'll start doubting yourself, and you won't have the proof in writing that you can do it.)

If you haven't seen any places where your skills would apply outside your current industry (or even if you have), this next step will force you to. On your list of skills, think of three other industries or functions that each one of those skills would apply to. If you can't think of three, write down the closest things you can. Again, don't worry about being right; this is still a brain exercise. The last thing your brain needs right now is anxiety. It's still in shock about the interrupted rest.

Step 3

OK. You now have lots of sheets of paper with all kinds of lists, and by now you're probably wondering where all this is going. Well, it's leading you to a place you probably haven't been to since you were a child. A place where, 'Let's pretend . . .' was still an acceptable way to start half the sentences you said and saying, 'Wouldn't it be great if . . .?' was something that you still applied to the daft ideas that popped into your head.

You are letting your creative side take over for a while. Instead of heeding the serious, follow-the-path voice in your head, you are listening to the you-could-do-this-if-you-wanted-to voice. For some people, they haven't heard that voice in a very long time. For others, they still hear it, but they've learned to ignore it. It's OK. I'm not going to tell you to run off and join the circus at this point. I just want you to understand that one of the biggest challenges in your job search is YOU. Without even realising it, you've been putting up obstacles at every turn in your job search.

The number one issue I see when people tell me that they're limited in their opportunities isn't a limited industry, it's a limited ability to recognise their options.

'Your industry isn't the problem. You are.'

On your last list, the one where you listed three industries for each skill, go through and copy all the industries onto a new sheet of paper. It's likely that there are several industries or roles that overlap or are very similar – that's good. Those are your *first-level targets*. (More about these later.) There are probably a random mixture of others that don't have anything in common. Those are your *second-level targets*.

Put all the other lists to one side for now – but don't throw them away, because you've already halfway through rewriting your CV with those!

Your list is now very nearly complete. What you have is a list of industries and roles that you can include in your job search. The next step will be to identify specific companies that match those fields and positions.

But first, we need to create a CV and covering letter that will sell you to those companies.

2. Day 2

The CV and Covering Letter

Before we go into writing your CV again (my guess is that you have at least three versions of your CV, but I wouldn't be surprised if the number was into the double figures. I've had clients who beat the 50-plus mark!), we first need to talk about the purpose of your CV.

You probably think your CV is a couple of sheets of paper designed to get you a job. Well, you're right, but only in the sense that you think petrol makes your car go. If you were given the job of building a V8 engine from scratch with only the concept that you need a block of metal that takes petrol in and makes your car go forward, you'd end up with something a lot less effective than if you understood that a V8 engine is an internal combustion device that utilises the compression of ignited petroleum to force pistons up and down to rotate a crank that spins a shaft that engages a ring and pinion gear that turns wheels, that . . . Believe it or not, your CV performs a task that is just as complicated. However, it's very likely that yours doesn't do it as powerfully as the one we are going to create together. Right now you have a single cylinder, two-stroke go-kart – or at best, a four cylinder engine. (Nothing wrong with four cylinder engines. I had a car with one and as well as having real go, it was great on petrol, but you could forget about winning races – and your job search is a race, not a trip to the corner shop.)

Your CV isn't a solitary item. It has, quite often, been forced to go it alone, but in your campaign it will have a partner. That partner is your covering letter. This twosome works like a tag-team in wrestling: Your covering letter steps into the ring first, listens to the ref explain the rules, nods at the recruiting manager and then dives forward and tackles him by the legs. Once the recruiting manager is down, your covering letter rolls over, swings his hand out to his corner and his partner, your CV, stretches his hand out, fingertips barely reaching his partner's, and they tag. In comes your CV, pile driving the recruiting manager, still being held down by your covering letter, stunning him. Your covering letter slips under the ropes before the ref can call him, and your CV pulls the recruiting manager around and locks him into a figure four, holding his shoulders down until the recruiting manager gives up and the ref calls the match to you!

Sounds very aggressive, doesn't it? Sounds like a sales job? Seems over the top and not your style? Yes, yes, yes! It is aggressive; there are thousands of candidates as qualified as you looking for those same jobs. It is a sales job; nobody wants to employ a person who doesn't impress from the very beginning. It is over the top because paper is boring; the only thing exciting about paper is what you put on it! If you don't jump off the page, you are never going to be seen. The recruiting manager who reads your CV is busy. If there isn't something that catches his eye, and fast, he's going to throw you in the TBNT pile fast! (TBNT means 'Thanks, but no thanks'. It's where most of your CVs have been ending up so far because your CV wasn't doing the job.)

> 'Your CV and covering letter are the tag-team salesmen knocking door to door on your behalf.'

The thing that most people I talk to never realise is that your CV and covering letter are the sales tag-team that opens the door for them. They get the recruiting manager motivated to call you in. But they also do a lot more than that. In the past, you may have had enough CV power to get to that first step, so you were getting initial interviews. You thought you were doing quite well, but then . . . nothing. You called the person you had the interview with and he told you he was trying to schedule a time for you to meet with so-and-so. What happened? Your CV let you down. (Good news – it wasn't you. It was your dodgy CV!) Although the CV and covering letter are responsible for opening the door, they are also the only salesmen that hang around after your interview to keep on selling you. Maybe you had enough CV power to get the door open, and you did impress your future supervisor when she interviewed you. But now your supervisor has to go to her manager and convince him that you are the best candidate for the job. All your supervisor has to work with are her great impressions of you and a weak, underpowered CV that doesn't help her to sell you to her manager. His boss, who is much too busy to look at bad CVs, shrugs off your supervisor, tells her she has a meeting to go to and to check back with her later . . .

Another opportunity lost, thanks to a bad CV.

Human Communication: The Basics

Now you understand how important your CV and covering letter are. Next you need to understand how they work. To revert back to my bizarre analogy of a CV-is-an-engine, it's now time to learn the theory of the combustion engine. How is petrol converted to horsepower? This is a lesson in human communications. Don't panic. There won't be any grammar lessons here. Instead, what we will discuss is how we human beings talk to each other. When my past client, Gary, ran into an old school friend at the supermarket and his old mate asked Gary what he'd been up to for the past 20 years, do you think Gary replied this way?

'I got married to Sylvia.

I fathered two children, Eric and Mandy.

I bought a house.

I purchased a BMW, silver.

I worked at XYZ company.

I was responsible for maintaining the budget.

I got made redundant.

I am now seeking to maximise that experience in a challenging new company.'

(Imagine this in an odd monotone voice. Would Gary's old school friend look at him strangely, or would he walk away quickly, then start running?) Sounds bizarre, but that's exactly how Gary's CV read when I met him. What about yours?

It's more likely that Gary would respond like this: 'Things are going well. Remember Sylvia, from our year at school? We got married. It's been almost 15 years now. We had two kids, twins, Eric and Mandy, they're both in their first year at our old school – going through the same things we went through! Sylvia and I bought a house in Rosebush Gardens a few years ago, did the whole BMW yuppie thing we said we'd never do. I was working over at XYZ as the Site Manager until they moved the operations abroad. Now I'm looking for something else. What about you?' (Same stuff, only now Gary's old friend thinks he's a successful man in transition, not a boring bloke who can't communicate.)

> 'How do we communicate in life? Stories. So why do we forget that in our CVs?'

The trick to effective communication, on the street, in a letter to your loved one, or on your CV, is to tell a story. That's how we human beings communicate. A truly powerful CV speaks to the reader in a story telling format. Your CV has to tell the story of your career. (Just your career, nothing else – no hobbies, no family life, no social issues. Those are all personal and have no bearing on your career whatsoever.) It tells the story of your career succinctly and with the best possible light shining on it. Why? Because that's how the person reading it will best be able to absorb what you're telling him or her, and that's how you make the reader *remember you*! If the HR manager were to read a list of bullet points about you, he would have forgotten the first bullets by the time he got to the last bullets. We just don't process information that way.

Creating a CV in a story format is easier than you think. The first thing to understand is that you won't be writing an autobiography. Unless your name is Bill Gates or J.K. Rowling, nobody will be interested enough to read more than a page or two of your life. Your CV is going to be a story written in what I call 'CV-ese'. It's similar to legal-ese, only there aren't any 17th-century 'shalls' and 'thereuntos'. The story we will be writing will be brief and to the point, with all the unnecessary prepositions and adjectives taken out. It will be just on the right side of stilted, but only to keep it succinct. And for you bullet-heads out there, I have some good news: We will be using some bullet points!

Before we go into the CV, we need to talk a little more about its tag-team partner, the covering letter.

'Why Are You Bothering Me?': Your Covering Letter As The Agent For Your CV

First, a little warning: I am about to mix metaphors again. Yes, your covering letter is the tag-team partner of your CV, but it also has a secret side job. Unbeknown to your CV, who thinks it's the star of the show, your covering letter is the real star. It's the brains behind the act. It's the agent that goes out there and books the gigs. It approaches HR managers and explains why you could be a great addition to the team. The first thing that the HR manager will read when your tag-team lands on his desk will be your covering letter. And the first thing this busy person wants to know is, 'Why are you bothering me?'

It's showtime for your covering letter. He has to give the 60-second pitch. I call this the 'elevator speech' because he has one minute to win them over. Your covering letter has one minute to answer four very important questions:

1   Why are you bothering me?
2   Why should I consider you for that?
3   If you're so great, why are you looking?
4   OK, how much do you want?

Sixty seconds.

Relax. You aren't going to start out writing the covering letter. As a matter of fact, the covering letter is pretty much going to write itself. Now it's time to jump in there and start writing the best CV you've ever had!

The Six-Pack CV: Creating A Position Build-Up In A Story

I don't know about you, but I am completely overwhelmed with the prospect of writing this CV. Only joking. I'm not, but you probably are. (Sorry, I have a mean streak. But I am also a big fan of KISS. Not the rock group, but rather, the old adage of 'Keep It Simple, Stupid'.)

I'm going to tell you what's going to remove all the pressure of writing the best CV you've ever had: your CV is only a tiny little story, repeated over and over until you get to the beginning. Each job you've had or each role you've had within the same company will be treated as its own little story. And each one of those stories breaks down to six simple little questions you're going to answer.

Phew! That doesn't sound very hard, does it? Who can't answer a few questions about their last job? (You WILL start with your last job FIRST on your CV. I don't care what anyone has told you about how you should write your CV; the HR manager wants to know what you have done recently, not what you did in your glory days 10 years ago. Whether you're a seasoned executive with more than 30 years of work history or a brand-spanking new employee in the workforce, the person reading your CV is most interested in finding out what you were doing before you came to them.)

'Keep It Simple, Stupid!'

We are going to take each one of your jobs – from now on I'm going to call them 'position build-ups' – and treat them as separate stories. I'll teach you how to write the first one, then you just repeat the process for each previous position build-up in your career until you come to the beginning, your education. (Again, I don't care what you've been told in the past, your education belongs at the end of your CV – unless you just graduated from university and have never had a job in your life. In that case, start with your education, and then treat any placements, part-time jobs, or university projects/theses as position build-ups.)

The six-pack CV

Six simple questions need to be answered in your CV. (Yes, everything in your covering letter and your CV is an answer to a question. You're playing *Who Wants to be a Millionaire?*, only this time you get to be Chris Tarrant, you get to know all the answers, and the recruiting manager is the contestant trying to beat the clock. Finally, you have the smug little smirk, read the correct answer from the screen, and act as if you knew that before you read it!) Get ready, here's your entire CV in a nutshell:

1 How/why did you get the job?
2 What was the situation when you got there?
3 What were the obstacles you had to overcome/goals you had to work towards?
4 What did you do to overcome those problems/reach those goals?
5 What were the results you got?
6 Why did you leave that successful job?

Not much to it, is there? It really is a very straightforward little story. The first thing you want to do is tell the reader how you got the job. Were you employed off the street, did they recruit you away from a more successful competitor, or did you get promoted from caretaker to facilities manager because you saved the company lots of cash by switching to better value toilet paper? Impress the reader with how you came to be in that job. (At no point in your CV are you to be modest. This is not the time or place for that. Modesty is for later, around your new colleagues, so they don't get sick of you.)

Your CV is the place where you put in all the action words and slightly extravagant adjectives you were always told not to use! Next, tell the reader what the situation was when you came on board. Was the company about to fall apart and you were the one responsible for sorting things out? Were all the customers unhappy and unsure that your company could fulfil its promises because of a history of late delivery and poor quality? (Don't paint too bleak a picture, unless that really was the case. It's OK to say that you were brought in to maintain a 20-year history of steady growth or to keep the department running smoothly. That still explains the situation and later when you tell them the results of your efforts, they'll have an accurate picture to compare it against.)

Once the reader understands the general condition of things, briefly outline what your primary objectives or obstacles were. Don't feel compelled to list everything you ever had to do or overcome at that job. Just the top one to three of them, depending on how complicated those things were. Remember KISS! (Maybe a picture of Gene Simmons near your computer would be helpful?)

Now the reader knows what you were supposed to do, it's time to tell him what you did. What things did you change or put in place to meet your objectives? Did you create a new team to address a problem, or write a new manual to clarify the issues? Maybe you just went and sorted it out yourself? Whatever they were, explain the main thing(s) you did to accomplish your mission.

Once you have told the reader how you got the job, what you were supposed to do, and what you did, NOW you share the results. These are the 'wow' items. Quantifiable results are best. (Think numbers: increased sales by 80%, saved the company £700,000, generated 50 billion new customers, and so on.)

This is the place to use those bullet points. Results look great as a bullet point, *if* you have explained how you came about them in advance. Now, just repeat this same little story for every job you had and remember to treat each role you had in the same company as a separate job. It demonstrates your progression within that company as well as your career. Don't be afraid to say you were promoted to lots of new jobs; it demonstrates to the reader your meteoric rise.

Format dos and don'ts

One more thing before you jump in there and finally write your masterpiece: the nuts and bolts of formatting. I won't tell you that there is only one way to format a CV, as I have seen lots of things that work, but I have seen even more that don't. (More information on don'ts can be found in Chapter 10. In this chapter we're only going to focus on the things that you *should do*.) This is more about what to include and what not to include. (For help on doing the formatting on your computer, ask a friend or pick up a 'dummies' guide' to MS Word.)

Name: Yes, do put your name on the CV and covering letter.

I have actually seen CVs that didn't have a name on them. Apparently, some people are concerned that people will find out they are looking for work. I suppose that means that they don't

want the person reading their CV to actually contact them, they
just want to tease the reader with the fact that someone out there is
watching them . . .?

Contact information: Include it.

Full contact info at the top of page one and a footer on subsequent
pages that includes at least your last name and a contact number.
(So that if the pages of your CV get separated, and the recruiting
manager sees something on page two that excites her, she can still
get hold of you!)

Summary statement/goal/objective: DON'T BOTHER!

Do you have any idea how many of those I have read? (More than
10,000.) Do you know how many of them were unique? (NONE!)
It's a waste of space. The only person who has a legitimate reason for
wanting a summary at the top of your CV is a recruitment consultant,
and that's just so he can easily fit you into the right section in his
candidate database. (More on that in Chapters 10 and 12.)

Company name: Do include it.

Also, include a brief description of what that company did. Even
if you worked for IBM, it's unlikely the reader will know what your
department did. Don't leave him or her guessing.

Your job title: Include it.

Even if your one and only task at your last job was to sweep the
floors, you had a job title. Caretaker, Facilities Assistant. Don't lie, but
give it the best spin possible.

Dates of employment: YES! Full dates, with months!

Always include the dates you worked at a company and always
include the months, as accurately as you can. Why? Because if you
don't, the reader will assume that there are gaps, and the reader is a
very cynical person. If you say you worked at XYZ Ltd from 1980 to
1990, and EFG International from 1990 to 2000, without including the
months, the cynical reader will assume that you got fired in January

1990, went to prison for six months, and, when you got out, you couldn't find another job until December. That's a whole year's gap when you were unemployed and in prison!

Hobbies: DON'T include them.

Think about it. Would you want to employ someone who told you on his CV that he has a hobby that takes up a huge portion of his time? Would you want to employ a person who says he is into skydiving? That means every weekend, he will be going out and trying to kill himself! Unless your hobby is working late every night, there is nothing in your extracurricular life that will help you get a job!

Personal data: NO, no and no!

First, this raises legal issues for the employer. Equal Opportunity laws prohibit an employer from making a decision about recruiting a person based on race, religion, background, and so on, and here you are trying to force that down the employer's throat. He would be better off throwing your CV out and pretending that he never saw it than to wade into that mess. Secondly, what could you tell him that would improve your chances of being recruited? That you have kids? Great, you'll be calling in a lot to take care of poorly kids. You're in good physical condition? Uh oh, methinks he doth protest too much . . . must have an undiagnosed heart condition and he's trying to sneak onto our health insurance scheme. References: no, don't include them and don't say you have them 'upon request'. The reader will naturally assume that you have someone out there who will vouch for you if asked and will, of course, know that you will provide them when asked.

✓ Your Day 2 Assignment

Step 1

Go through your current CV(s) and look for the answers to your six questions in each of the position build-ups you already have. Hopefully some of those questions have already been answered, but I wouldn't be too surprised if you came up empty-handed. (Your responsibilities at that job DO NOT count! By telling the reader what your responsibilities were, you are only telling him what the job was, not what you did there. You will do a good job of defining the position, which is great if your goal is to help your last boss get a better grasp on what your replacement will be doing, but completely useless if your goal is to demonstrate why you were successful in your previous jobs.)

On a blank sheet of paper, list all your jobs, starting with your most recent position first. (Remember to separate out different roles/titles within the same company.) Under each of those companies make a list, 1 to 6. These are the six elements of your position build-up. For each one of those questions that you already have an answer to, write it down next to the corresponding number.

Reminder of the six questions to answer

1 How/why did you get the job?
2 What was the situation when you got there?
3 What were the obstacles you had to overcome/goals you had to reach?
4 What did you do to overcome those problems/reach those goals?
5 What were the results you got?
6 Why did you leave that successful job?

Now, where are the missing pieces? In each one of the position build-ups, there are going to be missing answers. Don't tell me there aren't, because there are ALWAYS missing answers. If you had all the answers in your CV already, you wouldn't be reading this. You'd already be in your next great job! Go through your files, and get the answers. If you don't keep records of your past employment, now is the time to kick yourself for not doing it and to start keeping records. In the meantime, scrounge around through the dark dusty parts of your brain for the missing information. It's in there; you've just stopped looking at it. While you're digging around in there, make sure to also write down the dates that you were at that job. Be as accurate as possible and, for goodness sake, include the months. If you were in prison or simply unemployed for extended periods, note those in your time line, and we'll talk about how to deal with that later.

Once you have all the questions answered, you are ready to move on to Step 2.

Step 2

Put it together. Remember that you're telling a mini-story in the first paragraph(s). NO BULLET POINTS here! Basically, all you are going to do here is tell a very brief story of how you got the job, what the problems were, and what you did to resolve them. Then you put in some bullet points. After the bullet points (your achievements), end with your reason for leaving, EXCEPT in your most recent position. You don't need a reason for this one because your covering letter will explain that, and you may still be employed there (or at least you want to give the impression that you are still working or have just recently left).

Whenever possible, make the most recent position dates 'Month/ Year to Present'. An employed person is always more attractive to an HR manager than an unemployed person. That is just an unfortunate – or fortunate, depending on your circumstances – fact of life. When you're working, you are perceived as being more successful, and everyone wants a successful person on their team. If you aren't working and haven't for quite some time, it's not the end of the world, but you will need to do a little more work on the covering letter, giving a good spin on why you have been out of work for a while. I am going to give you a little example of how a position build-up should look. Feel free to borrow my style of CV-ese writing because, as you know, imitation is the most sincere form of flattery!

Example of a position build-up

XYZ Ltd
Anytown, UK
£10 million widget manufacturer.
January 1899 to June 1999 – Assistant to the Managing Director

Employed by the managing director to lead the anticipated growth of the department from a single widget manufacturer to a world-dominating widget superpower. Analysed and replaced antiquated widget assembly machinery to streamline production, while interviewing existing staff to determine their strengths and weaknesses. Wrote a comprehensive plan to achieve the predicted growth, recruited a leadership team to oversee new processes, and trained new and current staff on revised procedures and methodologies.

- Achieved growth goal six years ahead of schedule, under budget.
- Generated £30 million in annual savings with new machinery.
- Reduced production delivery delays by 75% by streamlining processes.
- Noted as being the 'best employee to work with' 12 years in a row by colleagues.
- Left to accept career growth opportunity as Chief Executive of Vodafone.

Keep doing this until you come to your education, then stop.

Step 3

It's time to write that covering letter. Good news: It's already done, you just have to find it! A quick recap: your covering letter has four little questions of its own that it needs to answer – and remember, it only has 60 seconds to do it, so remember KISS. Keep It Simple, Stupid.

Reminder of the four questions to answer

1 Why are you bothering me?
2 Why should I consider you for that?
3 Well, if you're so great, why are you looking?
4 Ok, how much do you want?

In a blank document (or on a blank sheet of paper), jot down two or three titles that you worked out in yesterday's homework that you were a good fit for. If they are unrelated or only apply to a certain industry that is different from the first, then you have a reason to write more than one covering letter. If, on the other hand, you have two or three job titles that fit you, and they are consistent across industries (HR administrator or sales manager, for example), then you only need one covering letter for your campaign. Next, go through your newly written CV and choose three to five bullet points that demonstrate that you have been successful in this type of role in the past. Cut and paste those into your new document or write them down. Now explain briefly why you are looking for this job. Are you looking to advance your career, did you just move to a new city, or did you get made redundant when the widget plant moved to Tibet?

OK, it's time to bite the bullet. Your next step is to tell them how much money you want. This is sometimes the scariest part for some people. Trust me: this will help you much more than it will hurt you. The last thing you want is lots of calls for jobs that pay half what you need just to make ends meet. Give them a range. Don't go mad and ask for a lot more than you're worth, and don't get stupid and undervalue yourself. (Too much and you knock yourself out of the running, too little and you appear as though you're 'damaged goods' – something must be wrong with you if you'll take that much of a pay cut.) You want to propose the salary in a range for a couple of reasons. One, it shows you are flexible and willing to negotiate, and people like to negotiate. Two, it actually gives you a much broader range of pay than you realise. For example, if you said you were looking for

£24,000 to £31,000, the reader could have a budget of £21,000, and feel that he would have a reasonable chance of getting you on board by adding benefits and a potential year-end bonus that would get you to your asking price. On the other side, if the HR manager has a budget of £35,000, and he sees that in recent years you've been making close to that, he knows he wouldn't be wowing you by offering you that, but would definitely be able to impress you enough to get you on board fast.

Lastly, after you have answered all the reader's questions, it's time to get things going. End with a strong 'Call to Action'. Guess what? You've finished this stage! Move on to the next step, but first, take the rest of the day off. You deserve it.

3. Day 3

Who to Get in Front of and How

How many pieces of junk mail do you get a day? Why do they keep sending them to you? Are they daft? No! Companies wouldn't carry on spending millions of pounds a year sending you junk mail if it didn't get results! The average direct marketing mailer is SEVEN pages long. Why do they send such a large amount of data and spend that much money? Because it works. Quite often when I talk to potential clients, the first thing they say when I explain what my company does is, 'That sounds like a shotgun approach'.

Instead, I explain to them that a 'shotgun approach' would be to post their CV to every Co-op and petrol station in their town, regardless of the position they were looking for. I then go on to explain to them that there are more than 2 million companies in the UK. That's right! If they sent their CV to that many companies, they really would be blasting away! But, that would be bonkers! Most of those companies would be a poor match for them either because of size or location or industry.

So, when I explain to my potential clients that we are going to look at that list of 2 million companies, and then select the few hundred that are a genuinely good fit for their objectives, they begin to realise the mistake in their thinking. (Or, they don't realise it, at which point I wish them continued success in their job search and get off the phone!) I am NOT going to tell you to bombard the country's companies with your CV. I'm not advocating a shotgun approach. What I am going to do is discuss how to turn your CV mailing into a campaign that uses a targeted approach to focus in on the right targets. The key to generating lots of activity in your search is EXPOSURE. Remember: there isn't a 'hidden job market'.

'The only thing hidden is YOU!'

When I work with my clients to develop a great list of companies for them to send their CV to, we discuss four main things:

1 Geography
2 Jobs and titles
3 Salary requirements
4 Industries.

Those are the key elements of what makes a great list for your job search. Remember Gary, the plant manager? He had been looking for work for more than six months and had only found 42 companies to send his CV to. After I worked with him, we found 498! That was because we developed a marketing plan before we developed a list.

Developing Your Marketing Plan

You've got a great product (you) and great marketing materials (your CV and covering letter). Now *who are you going to send them to?* If you were the director of marketing at a big company in Corporate Britain, and your boss came to you with the latest and greatest product that the company had to offer and he told you to come up with a marketing plan to sell it, do you think he would be impressed with the plan if it resembled your current job search?

- Putting lacklustre brochures about the product on websites where EVERY ONE OF YOUR COMPETITORS is posting an IDENTICAL brochure!
- Calling your friends and family and asking them if they want to buy your new product or if they know of anyone who does?
- Sending letters to independent sales agents, hoping that they will ask some of their customers to buy your new product (or the product of one of your competitors, because they represent them as well, and it doesn't matter to them which company they buy the product from – the agents will still get their commission!).

It's very likely that your boss wouldn't be pleased with this new campaign. In fact, he might encourage you to look for a new career and, to help you out, he'd probably throw in a couple weeks of severance pay to get you on your way. Sounds silly, but it's the same marketing plan you've been using so far. The key to a successful sales campaign is the same as it is for a great job search: know your target audience, find the right 'buyer' within that market, get in front of ALL of them and wow them with your product! You already have a great CV and covering letter, because we did that yesterday in Chapter 2. And we already have a list of the transferable skills you've accumulated throughout your career, as well as the industries that would respect those skills. So now it's time to go out there and apply all that work to a list. Don't get stressed; it's not going to be as hard as you think. You already know what you need. All you have to do now is learn how to get what you want.

There are a couple of ways to develop a list: you can buy one or you can create one. Obviously, it would be less work to buy one, but it would also cost you money to buy one. That might pose a problem, if you are unemployed and money is tight. It also might be hard for you to do if you're one of those people who are convinced that you shouldn't have to pay for a job. I get that argument all the time when I talk to people. They tell me that they wouldn't 'pay for a job' and that they would rather let a recruitment consultant find them a job than pay me to help them. We will look at how daft this view is later on but, for now, just be aware that even when I charge a client £2,000 for my services, I am charging anywhere from £8,000 to £35,000 *less* than a recruiter! Plus, you are spending astronomical amounts of your money for a job every day they're looking and you're still unemployed. Think about this: a person who makes £35,000 per year spends £680 per week in lost income for every week he or she looks for a job whilst unemployed! And he is essentially employing the least qualified person he knows to look for work – himself!

The other option for a list is to create one yourself. This can be inexpensive or even free (relatively speaking, building in the time you spend doing it and if there is lost income or not). The downsides of creating your own list are that, one, it's a lot of work, and two, it takes a long time. That may not be a problem, if you are looking for a better opportunity and you are currently working. But, if you are out of work, every second counts, and I would argue that the cost of a professionally created list far outweighs the cost of building one yourself. In either case, there are some things you need to know. You need to understand how mailing list companies work. These are the professional companies that generate lists. They accumulate information about every company and every person that they can find, and then they organise that information in many different ways so they can sell it to as many people as possible. These are the people who sell your name to the telemarketers and junk mail companies. If you have ever subscribed to a magazine or applied for a loan, credit card, mortgage, car, or even a contract mobile phone, they have your number. The same thing is true about every company in the UK.

List-compilers have a *lot* of information to organise and sell. They do this by using databases. One of the most important things to understand when compiling a list, either by using databases that are available across the net or when working with a professional marketing database company, is that you need to understand Standard Industrial Classification (SIC) codes. These codes are what mailing list companies use to identify types of businesses in their vast warehouses of business listings. The most important thing you need to know about them is: they're awful! But you still have to use them, so I still need to explain them to you.

SIC Codes

An overview

The first thing to understand about companies and lists is that they are all broken into industry classes. These are the main classifications:

A   Agriculture, forestry and fishing
B   Mining and quarrying
C   Manufacturing
D   Electricity, gas, steam and air conditioning supply
E   Water supply, sewerage, waste management and remediation activities
F   Construction

G Wholesale and retail trade; repair of motor vehicles and motor cycles
H Accommodation and food service activities
I   Transport and storage
J   Information and communication
K Financial and insurance activities
L   Real estate activities
M Professional, scientific and technical activities
N Administrative and support service activities
O Public administration and defence; compulsory social security
P   Education
Q Human health and social work activities
R   Arts, entertainment and recreation
S   Other service activities
T   Activities of households as employers; undifferentiated goods and services producing activities of households for own use
U Activities of extraterritorial organisations and bodies

When you look at it this way, it all seems fairly straightforward. If you keep your search to the major classifications, it IS quite easy. It's when you want to get a little more specific that you'll have to do some digging. That's because these major groups are just the tip of the iceberg.

Where it all started

The Standard Industrial Classification (SIC) Codes were first introduced in the UK in 1948 to classify businesses and other units by the kind of economic activity they were involved in. They followed the principles of the International Standard Industrial Classification of All Economic Activities (ISIC) which was issued by the United Nations. A European Community regulation required members to introduce a new Standard Industrial Classification SIC (92) to establish a common statistical classification. There was a minor revision in 2003 and a major international update of all industrial classifications, which started in 2002 and was completed in 2007, called SIC (2007).

As a result of the 2007 update, the classifications have increased from 514 to 615 separate classes, creating 101 new classes for newly recognised economic activities! There are now clearer distinctions between the service industries. The higher the level of the sector, the easier it is to obtain information about the sector.

Basically, they broke down all the economic activities going on in the country, shoved them into broad groups, and then broke those major groups into narrower sub-groups. They then took these new codes (which some would argue were somewhat confusing to the uninitiated) and handed them to the business world with the instructions to identify themselves within this system, and report back with their new SIC codes for their primary and secondary lines of business. Good luck.

Any organisation registered as a limited company or a charity at Companies House is allocated a sector. The code also applies to any VAT registered organisation or company with at least one employee. Here's how it works: a computer company, building and selling home computers for personal use would be in the major group of Section C: manufacturing, and then in Subsection DL: manufacture of electrical and optical equipment. You would then be in the sub-group 30: manufacture of office machinery and computers.

Great! Now you completely understand SIC codes, we're ready to move on. (Don't worry: The Further Information chapter gives a link to the ONS website, which carries a full explanation and the up-to-date list.) These index codes are just the first aspect of the list you are going to be putting together.

Location, Title And Salary

When you talk to mailing list companies, they will ask you lots of questions, trying to work out what you want. They are asking for information that they will then convert into database language (the details they need to be able to go out and find companies that match your criteria). If you're thinking about creating a list on your own, these are the same questions you should be asking yourself.

The first thing mailing list companies will talk about is the geographical area you want to cover. Most of them can look geographically in a number of ways (by postcode, city or county; some can also look in a radial search around a centralised postcode). So, work out where you want to get a job. Are you staying local and do you have to go home for lunch every day? (If so, be prepared for a long, uphill job search.) Is relocation something you would consider for the right opportunity? If so, where *would* you move, and where would you *never* move in a million years? How about your spouse? Would he or she kill you if you came home and said, 'We're moving to Leicester'?).

Another factor in your list is the size of the company. When you're looking for your next employer, keep this in mind. Will they be able to afford the salary you want? (A small family-run business only doing about £700,000 in sales a year, is probably not going to be able to afford to pay you £70,000 a year to keep the books or manage the office.) Also, think about the role you want to play in a company. If you think you should be at least a vice president or above, and the biggest company you've ever worked for only did £35 million in revenues, don't send your CV to Richard Branson suggesting that you would be a great manager of operations for Virgin!

You can still send your CV to that family run business, and you can still write a letter to Richard Branson – just set your expectations accordingly. The trick to working out the size of companies to approach is to have a solid grasp of what your objectives are: how much money you want to make and what role you want to play in a company. Then use your own experience or the knowledge/experience of the list broker to determine what size and location-type of companies you should be looking for. Location-type refers to the fact that most managed/compiled lists break down company locations by type (for example, headquarters, department headquarters, branch, or single location). Business lists are generally broken into the following types of categories:

- Technology-specific
- Industry-specific
- Title-specific
- Job-specific

One of the key things you will discuss with list brokers is the type of company you want to find. They may speak to you in plain English, but they will undoubtedly be converting it to SIC codes because that's how lists are managed. This is where all that company code mumbo-jumbo from earlier will be useful. Study the full SIC code list (details of where to find it are in the Further Information chapter). You should start making a list of relevant SIC codes before you call a mailing list company or thinking about doing the research for building a list on your own. You should be aware that mailing list companies use alternative codes – such as the Thomson Directories Classification, the Yellow Pages Classification – or even their own in-house system. But most use the SIC code too.

You could use the Thomson Directories Business Strata system as an alternative to mailing list companies. They feature more than 2 million business listings. You can find out more by visiting: www.thomsondirectories.com/directmarketing.aspx

'It's Not WHAT You Know, It's WHO You Know.'

Getting 'The Fear'

Last year I had a client named Andy who was a very likeable person. He was in his late 40s and had been methodically working his way up the corporate ladder throughout his career. He was now at controller level in his current company, but he had been stagnating there for several years. He originally got the promotion seven years ago and had not moved up since. His current boss, the Chief Financial Officer, was one of the founding members of the company, and he would not be letting go of the reins until he either retired (or, more likely, died at his desk!). Andy was getting restless and wanted to go out into the world to see if anyone else would have him. He asked my company to identify other businesses that would respect his abilities and give him the career path he deserved.

We came up with a great list of companies – around 800 altogether. His CV was superb (light years ahead of the amateur Microsoft Word template CV he had been using), and he had a covering letter that clearly stated his goals and why he should be considered for a director of finance role. Everything was happening. We started up the presses, loaded the CVs into the machine, and produced the finished envelopes. The final letters were wrapped and delivered to Andy's door so he could take them to his local post office and get a local postmark. Next step, start fielding calls.

Until . . .

A few days after we delivered Andy's package to him, I got an urgent phone call. Andy was in a real panic. 'There's been a huge mistake!' 'What are you talking about?' I asked him. 'All these letters are addressed to the manager or chief executive of those companies! I can't send my CV to these people; they'll never look at me. This is all wrong!' I calmed him down as best as I could and explained to Andy that, although he may feel that he wasn't at the level in his career to be personally communicating with senior executives in huge companies, I knew that his track record and his experience justified getting him in front of people who were at the level where they could appreciate the impact he could make on their company.

Andy got 'the fear' because we were sending his CV so high up within companies. I get that quite often, and most of the time we aren't even sending the CV to the chief executive! The most important thing to understand is that you have to get your CV into the right hands, and those hands quite often are not the hands of the person you'll be reporting to directly. Quite often it's the person that your manager will be reporting to.

It can be intimidating to post your CV to someone much higher up than you in a company, but sometimes you have to do scary things to reap the rewards you want.

After Andy calmed down and I convinced him to go to the Post Office, I didn't hear from him for more than a week. When I finally did hear from him, I thought I was talking to someone else. His confidence level had gone through the roof! Not only had he generated activity from the mailer, he had actually received several personal calls from chief executives and managers! In fact, after a second lunch with the chief executive of a mid-sized company (almost £10 million larger than his current employer), the chief executive offered him the position of chief financial officer – and the £14,000 raise that came with it! No more of 'the fear' for Andy!

✓ Your Day 3 Assignment

Step 1

Time to create the list

Remember those sheets of paper (or electronic documents) that you completed on Day 1? The ones where you listed all your skills, and then put them together, finding the common themes among them and then looking for industries that would respect those skills? Those are exactly what you're going to use when you research the SIC codes for your list! Find them, go online and start looking up the SIC codes for your industries. Remember: don't get so specific that you end up with a full digit code. If you do, you obviously have your blinkers on as you look for your ideal companies. Look around with an open mind. Once you have a list of codes, you're ready to move on.

Step 2

It's not what you know, it's who you know. Now that you know what companies you're going to look for, the next step is working out who to look for in that company. At this point, it would be helpful to understand your place within a company's hierarchy. If you have never worked before, you might be a little vague on corporate structure. I recommend you go to this website, which does a decent job of explaining the dirty truth of Corporate Britain today and your place in it: en.wikipedia.org/wiki/Org_chart

You have to know where you'll fit into an organisation because the most important thing in your campaign, after getting your CV to the right companies, is getting it to the right person within a company. I say person because that's what I mean: a person, NOT a human resources department! If you go through all the trouble of creating a list, writing a great CV and covering letter and then putting a first class stamp on it, only to send it to human resources, DON'T BOTHER. They don't actively recruit people – they recruit on the request of their colleagues. They don't know what would add value to each department in an organisation. The best that is likely to happen is that your CV will be forwarded to someone else in the company who may be recruiting at that time but there is no guarantee this will happen.

Remember: your CV and covering letter have to get into the hands of the right person, the recruiting decision-maker who will be your manager or your manager's manager.

That's right, the person you need to send your CV to is your next boss. Makes sense, doesn't it? Then why haven't you been doing it? Two simple reasons. You've been programmed since school to think of the HR department as the place where you send your CV, and you don't know how to find out the name of the person who would be your boss in a company you've never been to!

Well, that's why people work with mailing list companies. They have the answers. (You can find this out on your own without them, it just takes a lot more time and effort.) The person you have to send your CV to is the person you would either be reporting to directly, or the person your new boss would report to. This person will vary depending on the size of the organisation and the type of company. You will either have to do some thinking, based on your knowledge of your industry, or rely on the experience of your mailing list company. Remember: When in doubt, go higher. It's a safer bet to put your CV in the hands of the chief executive of the company when you are looking for a director of sales position than it is into the hands of the current director of sales. He isn't going to call you for an interview; he's going to throw away your CV and forget he ever saw it. One look at your CV and he will immediately realise that you are his replacement!

Step 3

As I discussed earlier in this chapter, you have the option of creating a list on your own, and I will go into that in a little more detail in a moment. However, first I want to talk about pay-for lists. There are lots of companies out there with mailing lists to sell or rent. Just do a search online to see how many there are.

When you work with a mailing list provider, you have the choice of using completely automated lists online where you simply click and order a list or you can work with a real person over the phone.

Most companies recommend contacting them before you order for the first time anyway. And I would recommend using a live person for your first list. The reason I suggest this is because it will probably be cheaper in the long run. The person will be able to give you valuable insight into how to find the right companies, and they can make sure that you only get the information that you actually need. You have to understand that in the world of lists, every little piece of information you receive costs extra. Lists are usually made to order. Explain to the mailing list company what you intend to do and ask for his or her help in getting the right level of information, without going overboard and paying too much. Some companies offer a free sample of the mailing list you want so you can try before you buy. This may be worth doing though you may have to commit to spending some money before you get your free sample!

Make sure you've got a pretty solid idea of what you want before you call. Have your worksheet with the SICs, titles and sizes ready, because that's what they will ask you for. Again, get their input about SIC choices. After all, they do this every day.

Finally, be prepared to tell them what format you want your list in. The main choices are Excel, Comma Delimited (CSV), Microsoft Access and Text. I would strongly recommend either Excel or Comma Delimited, as Microsoft Word and Works both have very good mail merge packages that work seamlessly with Microsoft Excel.

Alternative sources for list information

The internet You wouldn't believe what you can find with Google. Try searching for the websites of companies in your area. You can create a good list of companies in your area by using the phone book or, even better, an online phone book like www.yell.com, then look the company up on Google. Go to the website and look for a corporate organisational chart, or you can sometimes find contact names on an 'About Us' page.

Business organisations Use your local chamber of commerce to find your next job. Both online and in person, it's a great way to find companies in your local area, or in a city you'd like to relocate to.

They won't have a deep list of contacts within a company, but they usually have a list of many of the companies in the area. You'll probably have to pay a fee for the information; chamber members usually pay less than non-members. Your local Business Link may also be able to provide you with details of businesses in your region. It's also worth considering paying a small amount of money for information from Companies House; they offer a DVD containing details of companies in specific business activities. A couple of things to be careful about here: the information only features the registered business address and may not necessarily have the names and job titles of the people you need to contact, so you'd need to do more legwork yourself.

Your local library Libraries are great for local and national resources. They have lots of subscriptions online, so you might be lucky and find a free list provider at the local library. Don't forget to ask the librarians for help, too – they'll know about all the helpful resources available.

Mining your network for something valuable

Make the most of your network. Don't ask if they know who is recruiting; ask them who the recruiting manager is at all the companies they know. Explain that you won't mention their name, just that you want to post those people a copy of your CV. Most of your network will simply be so happy that you might stop calling them that they will go out of their way to put together a list! Whether you put together a list with the help of a professional or do it on your own, the goal is to get that list together as soon as possible, because it's the last hurdle before we get to the fun part: printing, folding, stuffing and stamping. (Yes, it really is just as much fun as it sounds!)

Links For List And Directory Sources

Chambers of Commerce
www.britishchambers.org.uk
Access to regional Chambers of Commerce websites

Business Link
www.businesslink.gov.uk
Access to regional Business Links

Companies House
www.companieshouse.gov.uk
Information on UK business registered with companies house

Yell.com
www.yell.com
National Yellow Pages with company information

Thomson Directories, Business Strata
www.thomsondirectories.com/directmarketing.aspx

SIC codes list
Office for National Statistics (National Statistics Online)
www.statistics.gov.uk/sic

4. Days 4 and 5

Getting Your CV Out There...

Good morning. It's bright and early on day 4 of your job search. Today is the day you start rolling up your sleeves and getting some real work done! Up to now, it's all been brain work and, though that's hard work, it doesn't leave you covered in paper cuts with black toner marks all over your favourite shirt. For the next two days, that may very well be your fate unless you ask a professional to do the work for you. (We will discuss this later, but for now just be aware that, although it might seem as if doing this all at home will save you money, you might be surprised.) Printing, signing, collating, folding, stuffing, sealing, stamping. Say this over and over for the next 48 hours, because that's what you'll be doing!

Every one of those completed envelopes is going on an adventure. Very soon each one of them will arrive on the desk of a busy executive, ready to spring out of its envelope, pounce on him, grab him by the neck and tell him, 'Look at me!' This is when things start moving. Any readers thinking that this is the part they were going to ignore – well, you're not getting it. The greatest CV in the world won't do you any good if it isn't getting into the hands of the right people. You might as well stick it in a desk drawer and forget about it. If you're thinking it won't be so difficult for you because you're only sending it to the five or 10 companies that you've chosen as the perfect opportunity for you, you *really* don't get it.

This Is Marketing: The Basics

If you had invented a great new widget and you wanted to sell 100 of them before the end of the month, would you send a flyer to 100 people and wait for them to phone you with their orders? Would you go to 100 houses and ask them if they would like to buy your great new widget and expect to sell 100 widgets? Of course not. Everyone understands the basic principles of marketing. Why? Because we get marketed to every moment of every day. Companies know that they have to expose their product to as many people as possible, as often as possible, to generate an acceptable level of sales. The same holds true for job searching. If you think you are going to send your CV to the three companies in town that you would love to work for, actually believing that you'll get a job, you might as well also buy three lottery tickets, then go to a bar and start drinking because the draw's on Saturday and you've got a couple of days to kill.

I've said it before and I'll say it again: exposure is the key to a successful job search. That is exactly what we're going to be generating in the next two days: exposure – and lots of it. The main approach I discuss in this book is direct mailing with paper, envelopes, and stamps. I don't recommend using email as a way of contacting potential employers in the first instance for a number of reasons (which I cover in Chapter 10). Although email is cheap, quick, and basically effortless, it is also temporary, is not very impressive, and lacks personal attention.

Yesterday, you created a great list of companies and you identified the most appropriate person in that company for you to get your CV in front of. So today we are going to create something for you to send him! The process isn't difficult. It really isn't any different to writing a letter to a friend, sticking it in an envelope and posting it to him or her. It's just that you are going to do it several hundred times!

There are resources out there to make your job much easier. First, let's talk about the do-it-yourself methods, what to do, and what NOT to do.

Do-It-Yourself: The Dos And Don'ts

Paper

Step one in producing your postal campaign is paper. This is a critical step in the process, not just because you have to have something to print your stuff on, but because the type and colour of paper make a huge impact on your presentation. If you got an advertising brochure in the mail and it was printed on low brightness, recycled-content paper with an inkjet printer whose cartridge was running low, you probably wouldn't be very motivated to read about the product. If the product was anything more than a £1.50 chocolate bar to help the local school raise money, you'd probably also wonder to yourself what kind of person sent this to you. You wouldn't feel confident that the product was worthy of your time and attention, and it's unlikely that you would call the number printed in faded ink to find out more about it.

Again, this sounds like common sense, but it's obviously not because this is a kind of CV that I see ALL THE TIME. I also receive CVs printed on coloured paper. Sometimes it is very subtle and I don't get distracted by it, but more often than not, if the job-seeker went with colour, he did so because he was colour-blind and didn't realise he was sending a professional CV out on fuchsia paper. (At least I hope that was the reason.)

Bright colours are bad. They make the CV or covering letter hard to read. They reek of the amateur and inexperienced, not a good fit. Your CV should be printed on bright white paper. (If you absolutely must print your CV on a coloured paper, do not – I repeat, DO NOT – use bright colours. An off-white, or natural colour is OK, but not great.) The paper should be of good quality. By this I mean 80 to 100 gsm paper. (Nothing higher, as you soon get into card stock, and that is hard to fold and just looks silly. Also nothing lighter, as it starts to feel flimsy, similar to cheap copier paper.)

Copier paper is OK (if it is all you have or can afford), but not ideal. Please, PLEASE don't use recycled copier paper or paper with a brightness less than 98. The whole purpose of the mailing is to make a good impression and encourage someone to call you. Looking cheap and unprofessional will not help your cause, and you won't be saving a significant amount of money.

Covering letter and envelopes

I am separating out the covering letter and envelope paper from the CV because you should really use a contrasting covering letter and envelope paper. (By contrasting I mean don't use the same white paper for the covering letter that you used for the CV, or vice versa.)

I like to use a good quality paper, preferably with a water mark. The idea is to make it look as if you are using your personal stationery to write a personalised letter to the recruiting decision-maker. Go to your local office supply or stationery shop and investigate this. If it is too expensive – don't buy a dozen boxes of that posh paper they sell in packs of 50 – then try to find a ream of off white or light grey 90–100 gsm paper, and they should have envelopes to match.

Don't use envelopes with windows (the kind you get your phone bill in) or envelopes and covering letter paper that has borders around it. You immediately look like you're sending a letter to your mother or someone who is recycling their junk mail envelopes.

Printing

Once you have paper, you have to print something on it. Otherwise you'll be wasting stamps and posting blank sheets of paper to people. If you have a laser printer, you're streets ahead. If you have an inkjet printer, I would strongly recommend you stop right now and jump ahead to the part where I talk about professional printing services. Inkjet printers are not meant to print large quantities of documents. They are slow. Even at the highest settings, their print quality is relatively poor, and they go through ink at an alarming rate. Personally, I think inkjet printers are a total rip-off.

If you think you have to use your inkjet printer because you'll be adding colour to your CV or covering letter, STOP! Not only is it a waste of time and money, but it also screams 'amateur!' Colour borders, pictures (no pictures, especially not of yourself, as it just opens up a can of worms – equal opportunities etc . . .), colour logos – none of them belong on your CV. If you feel it really is important to have a colour logo of your qualifications or some other thing, weigh that against the £40 to £60 added cost because you'll go through at least two colour cartridges printing 500 CVs, 500 covering letters and 500 envelopes. (When you add one little bit of colour to a document, your inkjet printer uses the colour cartridge to create that and all of the black text as well. It sprays all three colours together to create the black! Some printers have a feature to prevent this, but not all, so you run the risk of using A LOT of expensive ink to put that lovely little colour logo on your CV.)

If you are determined to print with an inkjet, use the highest DPI (dots per inch) and do it in black only. Then, pop a DVD into your computer and prepare to watch a lot of films while you babysit the printer. On the other hand, if you have a laser printer, you might be able to get the whole project done with only one toner cartridge. However, add in a lot more envelopes, as most laser printers eat envelopes like they're Pringles ('Once you pop, you can't stop').

My company prints CVs on the front and back of the paper. We do this for a number of reasons. It uses less paper (you're less likely to lose page two when it's stuck to the back of page one), you don't run the risk of having an envelope that weighs too much and you look more professional. In the surveys my firm has conducted, recruiting managers said that they had an impression of greater professionalism and a more sophisticated document when the CV was printed on the front and back. I recommend you do this, too. It will save you money, and it looks good (assuming you used a high quality heavy paper as I recommended).

Mail merge

If you have a PC you probably have Microsoft Office installed on it. If so, great – you already have a great mail merge program built right in. If you don't have MS Office, then I would suggest you download Open Office (www.openoffice.org). It's free, it's about 120 MB, and it has just about every single feature as MS Office. Most of them are better, and, at no point do you support Bill Gates' lavish lifestyle. I can't make you a mail-merge professional with this book. But once you get the hang of them, mail merges are very easy to do, and it's incredibly easy to keep track of your progress. It will look as if you personally posted your CV and covering letter to the manager.

Envelopes

Envelopes are a tricky subject because there are a lot of things to consider. I will tell you what my company does, and I will leave it up to you to do what you feel most comfortable with. My company addresses the envelope to the specific recruiting manager by name and title, then by company name. We do this by using an inkjet printer and printing directly onto the envelope. We then put a first-class stamp on it.

We do this because it looks professional and clean. I strongly advise against using post labels. It screams 'mass mailing'. This is the same reason I will tell you never to use metered mail or bulk-rate postage. I don't care if you do save a few pounds by using your employer's postage meter. Not only is it unethical to steal from your employer, but it also tells the reader that he or she is just one of thousands to get this same piece of junk mail. Why did you go through all of this trouble if you're going to stick a 'Don't Read Me' label on the front of it?

Personal and confidential

I can see the pros and cons of using this on the front of your envelope. You would do this in the hope that it would get it past the 'gatekeeper' (aka personal secretary or assistant) and right into the hands of the manager. Maybe it does, and maybe it doesn't. I have had clients who have chosen to do this, and I have yet to see any real difference in the response rate. I haven't heard anything negative from using it either, so I'm going to stay neutral on this one.

Timing

Timing is a huge part of a job search campaign. In the general sense, there is little you can do to affect the timing. When your CV arrives on the desk of a recruiting manager, she either needs someone like you at that time or she doesn't. Not much you can do about that. But in a small way, there are timing issues that you can affect.

You can control when it lands on that person's desk – not with 100% accuracy, but at least to some degree. You don't want your CV to arrive on that busy person's desk on Friday afternoon, to be quickly forgotten in the rush to go home for the weekend, nor do you want it to land in the huge pile of 'weekend' correspondence that will inevitably overwhelm him or her on Monday morning. Ideally, you want your CV and covering letter to hit the recipient's desk mid-week (Tuesday, Wednesday or Thursday). This means if you are posting locally, don't send your CV on Thursday because, it's very likely that it will slide into the Friday free-for-all or crash into the Monday avalanche. Post on Monday or Tuesday if it's going local.

For a national search, the timing is a little more tricky. Add in an extra day for every 200 miles it has to travel. Another thing about timing while we're on the subject: dates. Never put a date on your covering letter! Just don't do it. There is no upside and many downsides. When you put today's date on your covering letter, you immediately give it a shelf life. It's like the expiry date on food packets. The same thing happens to CVs that have a date. If it lands on that recruiting manager's desk and gets shuffled to the bottom of the pile, the last thing you want to happen when it resurfaces a few days or sometimes a few weeks later, is for it to have a date on it that says to the reader, 'You're too late, throw this away!' If there is no date, it still looks fresh. Clients have told me they've received calls sometimes six months after they posted their CV!

Getting Professional Help (For Your Campaign, Not Your Personal Problems)

OK, let's assume you have finally added up the cost of the paper, the envelopes, the toner and inkjet cartridges, the repair cost for the broken printer, and the number of plasters you'll need for the paper cuts, and you have decided it's time to look into getting some professional help!

Stationery shops vs. printers

You now have a couple of choices. I can't tell you which way is better, because that really depends on the size of the mailing you are doing, the amount of 'sweat equity' you are willing to put into this part of the process, and how good you are at negotiating. But I can give you an idea of what two of the most logical options.

The two most likely sources for professional help are stationery shops and printers. Office supply or stationery shops include places like Staples, Ryman and the like. By print shops, I mean either the franchise printing shops where they use offset printing presses to whip out thousands of forms an hour (such as Prontaprint or Alphagraphics), or privately run print shops. They both produce excellent results, and they both have their advantages and disadvantages.

Stationery shops

I've done a little shopping, and I've got some rough prices from my local stationery shops. They all came in at about the same price range for their services. Not surprising, because they compete against each other on a daily basis. I have found that on average, you can get a CV printed on 100 gsm paper for about 10p per side. That means that, to print 500 double-sided CVs, it will cost you around £50. Not a small chunk of change by any means, but maybe not that expensive when you start adding up the cost of your inkjet toner cartridges.

The advantage of using this type of place is that once they have printed your CV, some of these places can also print your covering letter and envelopes. (They can do the actual mail merge for you.) The costs and the level of service vary. Some places will actually fold and stuff them, and some places will only do the printing and give them to you flat, so you can do your own final collating. The prices vary for this as well; the average that I have seen is somewhere between £20 and £50. At the end of the day you may have spent around £100–£150, but you will have finished your job search campaign and it will be ready to hit the post (once you attach the stamps!).

Printers

Quite often when I talk to people about printers, they seem intimidated by them. I think it's because most people have the impression that printers only do large jobs, printing thousands of copies of things at a time. Not true. Most print shops rely on small jobs to keep the lights on. However, some of the bigger chains no longer do this type of print job so contact them to check first.

Local print shops usually charge in the range of 4p to 10p per CV page and between 20p to 30p per envelope. So, 500 one-page, two-sided CVs and an equal number of envelopes printed with your return address would cost about £225. These places may also do mail merging.

✓ Your Days 4 and 5 Assignment

Step 1

Go shopping. Call your local stationery shops and check with the
printers in your area. Get a good idea of what the options are for you.
Then look at how much 'sweat equity' you want to put into this. If
you have family members who can help you (and are old enough to
do this without smearing chocolate on the letters and can keep them in
the right envelopes), you might be better off using a printer, taking the
whole thing home and having an envelope-stuffing party!

Step 2

Get it done! Take your stuff to the local printer or copy shop or
buy the supplies and start doing it yourself. Whatever approach you
choose, this is going to take some effort. Either the kind where you get
lots of paper cuts, or the kind that I hate even more – that is, the kind
where you have to drag your wallet out and pry it open.

Step 3

Stamp it and post it. As soon as you have your trays of envelopes
completed, whether you and your family did it or you just picked it
up from the printers, the last step is to stick stamps on them. A few
last words of warning: Do not use stamps that support a 'cause'.
Inevitably, if you use a stamp that supports AIDS awareness, breast
cancer, or Elvis, you are running the risk of turning people off before
they call you. Don't waste opportunities because of something as
inconsequential as a stamp. Use the generic first class stamp. It's
simple and it looks professional. Do not use metered mail or bulk rate
postage. I've said it before, and I am going to say it one more time:
DON'T DO IT.

I recommend that you take the envelopes to the Post Office instead
of dropping them into a post box.

That's it. The race is on!

5. Day 6

What to Expect, What Not to Expect, and Why

First Results: The Depressing Realities Of Direct Mail

Today is an exciting day. You just dropped your envelopes off at the post office. You are now sitting next to the telephone, ready to start taking those job offers! You're right to be excited, but you need a little reality check. You aren't going to get any calls today – right now the envelopes are going through the complex machinations of the British postal system. Even if you are posting locally, it will be at least a day before your CV lands on someone's desk. That's OK. It gives you time to get ready – time to get ready for the job offers, and time to get ready for some of the realities of a postal campaign.

One of the ironic things about the post office is that they are at their most efficient when they're admitting defeat. The first letters you will get will be the undeliverable ones. The first thing to understand about that mailing list that you used: whether you paid a professional or did every bit of the research yourself to create the list, it is not going to be 100% accurate. In fact, if it is 90% accurate, you have a very good list. That means that you should expect at least 10% of your letters to come back to you marked as undeliverable. Either the address has changed and the forwarding address has expired, the person you mailed it to is no longer with the company, or worse yet, the company has gone out of business. These things happen.

There is nothing that you or anyone else can do about it. The mailing list company has huge teams of people who sit in reading rooms, constantly going through company filings and trade journals, newspaper articles, and survey results, trying to keep up with the activity that occurs in Corporate Britain. They have telemarketing groups that regularly call companies to update the information on their databases. It's an ongoing battle. A large mailing company, like Dun & Bradstreet (D&B), may keep records on as many as two million companies in the UK. Companies try to collect as many contacts in those businesses as they can, with the number of contacts per company ranging from three to 10 contacts per company.

What does this mean to you? Well, it means you shouldn't get discouraged when a letter comes back undelivered. It also means you shouldn't get angry or silly about it either. Calling your mailing list company and demanding your money back would just prove to the world that you are unaware, unreasonable, and unlikeable. They don't guarantee 100% accuracy. No one does. That means you take the good with the bad. If you want to do a little more research, you can call the company that you posted your CV to (if they are still in business) and ask for an updated address or new contact person. Or you can move on and accept the fact that these things happen.

> 'It takes an incredible amount of rejection to generate a positive response.'

OK, undeliverable letters aside, let's move on to the next reality of direct mail: rejection. You are going to get Thanks, But No Thanks (TBNT) letters. As a matter of fact, you're going to get more TBNTs than calls for interviews. A lot more. If you had a 1% positive response rate on a mailing of 500 letters, you would only get five offers. Don't get me wrong: I'm not saying that five job offers is a bad thing! I'm just saying that along with those five offers, you'd be getting an average of 10% return to sender (or, put another way, 50 undeliverable envelopes). And you should expect at least 10% of the letters to land in HR, where they will generate a form TBNT letter, so that's another 50.

You do the sums. That means that for the five job offers, you have to put up with 100 rejections! Apparently getting a job is similar to publishing a book: It takes a lot of people telling you that you have no talent and will never amount to anything before someone comes along (such as my agent and my publisher) and says, 'Hey, you are

an incredibly talented person, and we'd love to have you on board!'
Shameless flattery, but it's true!

Thank-you Letters (Yours And Theirs)

I can't tell you how often my clients call me and ask if they should
send a thank-you letter to so-and-so. The answer is always yes.
Always. Etiquette gets you into more interviews than raw talent.
Look around you. How many times have you seen someone who was
obviously not very gifted or talented working at a better job than
you would expect? How many of those people were courteous and
friendly?

> 'Good manners can take you a long way in this world.'

It only takes a couple of minutes to write out a thank-you letter.
(I've included a few examples at the end of this chapter to make it
even easier for you.) The rewards far outweigh the effort.

So many clients have told me that they got a personal letter
from a recruiting manager at a company that we contacted,
saying that they were impressed with the client's CV, but they
just didn't have anything for them right now. Send that person
a thank-you letter!

You don't know what other opportunities might be lurking in a
recruiting manager's circle of acquaintances. A common scenario
I encounter is this: the recruiting manager sends a personal letter to
my client, and my client sends a thank-you letter back that lands on
the recruiting manager's desk a week later. Over that week, something
has changed at his company or with one of his supplier's/partner's/
friend's companies, and NOW my client would be a great match. He
contacts my client and another opportunity happens! Two or three
minutes and 39p to generate a job offer – not bad!

Networking Your New Contacts

Networking? New contacts? What are you talking about? I thought
I just had to sit back and wait for the magic to happen. Who are these
new contacts? I've been sitting at my desk for a week. Who have

I made contact with besides the bloke at the local copy shop? That's
right. There's more work to do. Looking for work is a full-time job.
If you think you only need to do this for an hour or two a day, you
will be taking a lot longer to find a job than you think. Just because
you've posted your CV to all the companies that you would like to
work for, the day isn't over. OK, you'll be getting some calls. You'll
also be getting some letters, good and bad. There's more to do than
just answer the phone and check your post.

'Looking for work is a full-time job.'

You now have a list of new contacts. You paid a great deal of money
for that list (either hard-earned cash or hard-earned sweat equity),
so you should make the most of it. I always tell my clients to use
the list for networking. What I mean by this is to pick up the phone
and start calling those companies. You have a perfect way in. You're
calling to follow up on a letter that you sent to Mr. So-and-so. Did
he get the letter? You're looking forward to discussing any potential
opportunities that might be available. Does he know of anyone else
who might be looking for someone with the great skill set you have?

Yes: cold-calling. Some people get ill just at the thought of picking
up a phone and calling someone they don't know. Others can't wait to
get up in the morning and start. Personally, I think it's awful, but I do
it. And those people you're talking to can't see you and you can't see
them. So if they reject you, how likely is it you'll ever meet them? Not
very. So what's the problem?

Personal letters from recruiting managers are a particularly good
source for networking. This is someone who was impressed enough by
what he or she saw to write you a note, so why shouldn't you call and
try to network with him or her?

'Get over your fears and phobias. Your biggest fear should be of not following every path to a great new job!'

Now Is Not The Time To Sit Back And Wait For The Action!

You've heard the old saying 'strike while the iron is hot'. Well, that branding iron is red hot, so you'd better get on with it! The time to generate job activity is all at once. The biggest mistake I see job-seekers making is taking the 'serial' approach to their job searches.

If you follow up on every opportunity to its bitter end before moving on to the next opportunity, you're going to be looking for a very long time. Going to a job interview, then waiting for a week to hear if they are going to call you back in, then waiting another week to find out if you got the job could very well end in three weeks being unemployed, with no prospects! I say no prospects because there is a very good chance that at the end of that three weeks, they tell you that they recruited someone internally. Now it's time for you to start all over again. How many times do you do that before your cash runs out?

> 'You've got to get on with it while the going's good.'

When you generate as much activity as possible in as short a time frame as possible, you end up in a situation where you are going to multiple interviews, and you'll be getting better with each one. Your confidence increases significantly when you're constantly talking about your strengths and meeting potential employers who are interested in you. It's that confidence that makes you attractive! The ultimate result of all of this activity, in a limited time period, is multiple job offers! When you have more than one job offer at the same time, you are in a unique position: you can now push one against another so that you can achieve your maximum market value. (More about this exciting concept in Chapter 8.) For now, you have to do a lot more work before the end of the day, so get on with it!

Phones, Voicemail And Answering Machines (And Why Your Kids Aren't Sweet)

A couple of things to be aware of before you start. You must have a professional attitude about your job search. The professionalism projects itself to potential employers and is partly what motivates them to take you on. That means you have to be prepared to answer the phone when it rings, ready to discuss yourself, your CV, and why you approached their company. Keep a list of the companies, their industry (their SIC code) and the person you sent your CV to right next to the phone, as well as a copy of your CV. Don't try to wing it when it comes to talking about your CV; you'll fail every single time and say something that contradicts what's there. Look at it while you discuss it. That thing is an outline of your career; it talks about all of your experiences and successes. Use it to your advantage.

If you don't have voicemail, get it. It has some big advantages over answering machines. The most important one is that it can answer calls even when you're talking to someone else. The worst thing to do is not answer a potential employer's call. Get call waiting. If you have teenagers in the house, get them a mobile. They'll love you for it, and your phone won't constantly be in use, causing you to miss opportunities. If you must use an answering machine, don't put a quirky little message on it! Getting your three-year-old to leave an outgoing message is fine if the only people you expect to call are the grandparents, but it's a very poor way to project your professionalism to a potential employer!

Phones and internet access

How many opportunities are you missing while you're surfing the net? If you are still living in 1998 and have a dial-up connection, either stop surfing, get a second dedicated line, or buy an internet call waiting device. I am constantly leaving voicemail for people only for them to call me back five minutes later to tell me they were online.

They think they haven't missed anything because they call straight back. Wrong! First, you've ruined your professional appearance.

Second, you might not be able to reach the caller because he is already talking to the number two candidate!

> 'You can't afford to miss a single opportunity.'

Use a mobile phone as an alternative contact number. Make sure your outgoing message is clear and says your name (so they know they called the right number), and check it frequently. If you miss a call, return it as soon as humanly possible. Don't get distracted by everyday tasks and put it off until tomorrow. If you can afford to miss opportunities to take care of little projects around the house, you can afford to retire.

✓ Your Day 6 Assignment

Step 1

Get your house in order. Re-record the outgoing message on all your contact numbers, making sure that it sounds professional, that you state your name, and that there aren't any children or flushing toilets in the background! Print out an abbreviated list of the companies that you posted your CV to, alphabetised by company name and line of business, making sure you include the name and title of the person you posted your CV to. Staple that list together and then keep it next to the phone at all times so you can quickly look through it and see who you're talking to. Keep a copy of your CV on you at all times. Fold one up and stick it in your wallet if have to. Don't try to talk about yourself without it. It's your back up for the biggest test of your career.

Step 2

Go through your list and choose the top 50 companies you would most like to work for. This is your first list to start calling. If you get through that list before lunch, make a list of the next 50 and start calling them. If you don't get through the list in the first day, you should be through it by mid-morning the next day. Otherwise you will be behind on calling companies 50–100, and then companies 100–150, and so on.

Step 3

Follow up. Remember: when in doubt, send a thank-you letter. Don't feel silly sending a thank-you letter to a thank-you letter. Thank-you letters and personal notes are an important part of the job search process. When you get a note from a recruiting manager, you now have a perfect way in to call him or her and network. Don't miss your chance!

Sample Thank-You Letters

General thank-you letter

Mr A. N. Other
Head of Customer Services
The Widget Company
1 Interviewing Street
Jobville
Anywhereshire
AB12 3CD

Dear Mr Other,

Thank you for taking the time to discuss the JOB TITLE position at The Widget Company with me. After meeting you and getting to know the company a little more, I am even more convinced that my background and skills are a great match for your needs.

In addition to my qualifications and experience, I will bring excellent working habits and a great attitude to this role. With so many demands on your time, I am sure you appreciate staff who can be trusted to undertake their responsibilities with minimal supervision.

I look forward to hearing from you about your decision.

Again, thank you for your time and consideration.

Yours sincerely,

Vernon L. Dent

Thank-you letter that tempts the employer

Ms A. N. Other
Head of Customer Services
The Widget Company
1 Interviewing Street
Jobville
Anywhereshire
AB12 3CD

Dear Ms Other,

I want to thank you for taking the time to interview me yesterday for the position of JOB TITLE of The Widget Company. You and Mr. Other Manager were very encouraging, and I know we could have a great working relationship. Looking at the job description for the role in more detail made me even more confident that I could take the organisation to new heights of success. With the resources I've gathered, I'm ready to hit the ground running with SPECIAL SKILL. The SALARY PACKAGE DISCUSSED is an excellent incentive, and I'm very motivated to deliver results. I am convinced I could bring a new degree of organisation to the company, including SOMETHING DISCUSSED IN INTERVIEW. More importantly, I'd like to get ANOTHER THING DISCUSSED IN INTERVIEW and I am committed to doing so.

Thank you once again for considering me for this position.

I look forward to working with you.

Yours sincerely,

Vernon L. Dent

Thank-you letter building on your strengths in the interview

Mr A. N. Other
Head of DEPARTMENT
The Widget Company
1 Interviewing Street
Jobville
Anywhereshire
AB12 3CD

Dear Mr Other,

I'd like to thank you for talking to me about the JOB TITLE position in your DEPARTMENT. I really appreciate all the time you took to tell me about the job and to find out more about me. I'm so pleased that you agree that my SPECIAL EXPERIENCE in RELATED ISSUE gives me a great level of experience for this role. I'm keen to bring my passion for this to the JOB TITLE position, and I am convinced the knowledge and experience I've already acquired make me the best candidate for the job.

I look forward to hearing about your decision soon. Please feel free to contact me if you need any more information about my qualifications.

Thank you, again, for the interview.

Yours sincerely,

Vernon L. Dent

Thank-you letter that emphasises your match with the company

Ms A. N. Other
Head of Customer Services
The Widget Company
1 Interviewing Street
Jobville
Anywhereshire
AB12 3CD

Dear Ms Other,

Thank you so much for taking the time to interview me today for the JOB TITLE role. I felt a great rapport with you and with the whole Widget Company staff. I am more convinced than ever that I will fit in well as a member of the team and contribute my skills and talents for the benefit of The Widget Company. I can make myself available for any further discussions of my qualifications that may be needed. Again, Ms. Recruiting Manager, I very much appreciate you and your staff taking the time to talk with me about this exciting opportunity.

Yours sincerely,

Vernon L. Dent

Thank-you letter with afterthoughts

Mr A. N. Other
Head of Customer Services
The Widget Company
1 Interviewing Street
Jobville
Anywhereshire
AB12 3CD

Dear Mr Other,

   I'd like to thank you for the time you spent talking with me about the JOB TITLE. I am very excited about this role and convinced that my RELATED EXPERIENCE equips me more than satisfactorily for the job. I meant to mention during the interview that last TIME I attended a SOMETHING on SOMETHING RELATED TO POSITION. I know the job description mentions the ability to use SOMETHING, and I wanted to make sure you knew that I have a great deal of experience in the use of this TOOL/SKILL.
   Please contact me if you have any questions about my ability with this or about any of my other qualifications. As you know, my PREVIOUS position in the PREVIOUS DEPARTMENT at PAST EMPLOYER gave me an excellent background for NEW JOB TITLE work. I look forward to hearing from you soon about the position and would like to thank you again for meeting with me.

Yours sincerely,

Vernon L. Dent

Thank-you letter with damage control

Ms A. N. Other
Head of Customer Services
The Widget Company
1 Interviewing Street
Jobville
Anywhereshire
AB12 3CD

Dear Ms Other,

Thank you for the time you took to interview me for the
JOB TITLE role. Following our interview, I'm now convinced
that I have the qualifications you're looking for in your JOB
TITLE. I know you expressed some concern in our meeting that
I have not worked in a SPECIFIC AREA. I want to emphasise,
however, that I have participated significantly in A RELATED
EXPERIENCE for PAST EMPLOYER and have a solid record
of achievement in RELATED EXPERIENCE.

As for your requirement for experience in SOMETHING
YOU DON'T HAVE, my having been SOMETHING
SOMEWHAT RELATED, along with outstanding
SOMETHING ELSE KIND OF RELATED, qualify me more
than adequately. Thank you again, Ms. Recruiting Manager, for
this interview opportunity for the JOB TITLE role. I know I
could make a great contribution to your company. I look forward
to the next step in the process.

Yours sincerely,

Vernon L. Dent

Thank-you letter for an on-campus recruiter

Mr A. N. Other
Head of Customer Services
The Widget Company
1 Interviewing Street
Jobville
Anywhereshire
AB12 3CD

Dear Mr Other,

Thank you so much for talking to me today about the role in JOB TITLE at The Widget Company. I am very excited about this opportunity. I am sure I have the energy and dedication it takes to be successful within your company. My education has equipped me for this job, and my enthusiasm will ensure my success. My internships with RELATED COMPANIES have taught me a great deal about meeting the needs of The Widget Company.

I would like to take the next step in this process and discuss the position further with you. I plan to contact your assistant on DAY to arrange a mutually convenient time to meet.

Again, Ms. Recruiter, thank you very much your time and the inspiration you gave me to launch my career at The Widget Company.

Yours sincerely,

Vernon L. Dent

Thank-you letter for a career/job fair

Ms A. N. Other
Head of Customer Services
The Widget Company
1 Interviewing Street
Jobville
Anywhereshire
AB12 3CD

Dear Ms Other,

Thank you for taking the time to meet with me at the NAME Career Fair today. I really appreciated your time and attention. You were very thorough in explaining The Widget Company's POSITION TITLE. Now that I have a better idea of what the role entails, I'm even more certain that I would be an asset to your team and to The Widget Company.

My solid education from YOUR University's SPECIFIC Department, and the fact that I have worked my way through university, show a strong work ethic and determination, two qualities you said were important for success at The Widget Company.

I look forward to an opportunity to visit The Widget Company and speak to you in more detail about the role. I will contact you next week to arrange an appointment.

Thank you, again, for your time and consideration.

Yours sincerely,

Vernon L. Dent

Thank-you letter for career networking

Mr A. N. Other
Head of Customer Services
The Widget Company
1 Interviewing Street
Jobville
Anywhereshire
AB12 3CD

Dear Mr Other,

Thank you again for agreeing to be a member of my personal 'network'. This is an important time in my life as I make the move towards changing careers, and I really value the advice of professionals like you who know the NEW CAREER field so well. I especially appreciate your offer to introduce me to other professionals and JOB TITLES in your network, which I know will be extremely helpful to me in establishing myself.

I'm very grateful to you for your willingness to help me launch this next phase of my career. I will keep you up to date with my progress. Please do not hesitate to contact me if you think of any other suggestions for expanding my network and establishing myself as a NEW TITLE.

Yours sincerely,

Vernon L. Dent

Thank-you letter after job rejection

Ms A. N. Other
Head of Customer Services
The Widget Company
1 Interviewing Street
Jobville
Anywhereshire
AB12 3CD

Dear Ms Other,

    Thank you for your consideration for the JOB TITLE position. While I am disappointed not to be chosen for the role, I learned a great deal about your company, and I enjoyed meeting you and your staff. I really appreciated the professional manner in which you conducted the interview.

    Please keep me in mind for the future. I have a strong interest in your company. I believe we could work well together, and I will be following the progress of your company closely over the coming months. Perhaps we will be in touch in the future.

Best wishes,

Vernon L. Dent

Thank-you letter to accept a job offer

Mr A. N. Other
Head of Customer Services
The Widget Company
1 Interviewing Street
Jobville
Anywhereshire
AB12 3CD

Dear Mr Other,

I am pleased to accept your offer, and I am looking forward to joining you and your staff TIME DISCUSSED. The JOB TITLE position is ideally suited to my background and interests. I will make the most of the role to benefit your company. I understand I will begin work on MONTH DAY, YEAR.

If, in the meantime, I need to complete any paperwork or take care of any other matters, please contact me on phone number. Thank you for this exciting opportunity, and I look forward to working with you and the rest of the team.

Yours sincerely,

Vernon L. Dent

6. Days 7–9

How to Handle the Interviews

Treat Every Opportunity As The Best Thing Since Sliced Bread

You've just spent a shedload of time, money and energy creating a successful job search. Now you have to concentrate on making the most of it! I can't tell you how many times I have worked with clients for weeks, putting together a fantastic CV, an attention grabbing covering letter and a faultless list. We post the client his envelopes, he takes them to his local post office and the letters hit the recruitment manager's desk. The recruitment manager is suitably impressed, picks up the phone and calls my client. This is a perfect scenario. You'd love to be at this point right now, wouldn't you?

Wait till you hear what my client does next. He takes calls from various companies. He asks them questions like, 'Where are you located?', 'What's the starting salary?' and 'Do your employee benefits start straight away?' You probably thinking these questions seem quite reasonable, so what's my point?

My point is that those are absolutely terrible questions to ask in a first phone interview! Awful!

Why? Because he asked questions that should be saved until after he's convinced them that he's better than sliced bread.

A first phone interview is a tricky thing. One wrong comment and the recruitment manager could think you are only interested in pay and benefits rather than a role within their organisation. That will be it. You will have lost what could have been a golden opportunity.

Now is not the time to decide if you want to move forward with this opportunity. You don't know if it's a good opportunity or not. You don't. Full stop. I don't care if it is a low-paying, entry level job for a sewer-cleaning company. The first phone interview is simply not the time to screen opportunities.

You must treat every call as though it's the best call. You need to make every person who calls you think that they are describing your dream job. The sole purpose of the first phone interview is to 'wow' the person on the other end of the line enough to motivate him or her to invite you in for a face-to-face interview. Your goal is to get your foot in the door of as many companies as you can. Why? Because you need practice. Practice at interviewing. Practice at selling yourself to multiple people a day. Practice making an impression as you turn to the second page of your CV and tell the interviewer how you saved this employer more than millions of pounds by installing reusable toilet paper dispensers.

I've worked with high level executives and 25-year veteran corporate sales trainers, and every one of them made more mistakes in the interview than a young graduate fresh from university. You don't know what you're doing wrong until someone tells you. We're going to discuss some of the mistakes you may well be making in a while – but first, you need some practice. That's your goal for the next few days: get as many interviews as you can. Get the practice in. The only way to get better at interviews is to practise. A lot.

The other reason to accept every interview that comes along is because you don't know where your next job will come from. You might walk into an interview for a project manager role, talk to the department head, and discover that he's having issues at another site.

The next thing you know, you're the plant manager starting up a new manufacturing operation. Think that sounds unlikely? That's exactly what happened to my client, Gary. He went to an interview for a position that he didn't feel was even a remotely good match for him. The manager who called him in didn't really think there was a fit for the position either, but he was impressed with his CV and was always on the lookout for talent.

After a face-to-face interview, where Gary spent a half hour selling himself on the basis of his experience of turning companies around, his new boss realised that this was just the guy to take a struggling business and turn it into a thriving profit centre. (Gary later told me that he didn't even want to go on that interview because he knew it was just a waste of time!)

Accept EVERY Interview Offered

There are to be no wasted opportunities. If you are unemployed and you turn down an interview, you're making a mistake. Every time you say thanks, but no thanks, to an HR director who is calling to pre-screen you for a job you're not interested in, you're selling yourself short. Accept every interview, regardless, until you are employed, happily employed, and completely sure that you are not going to need another job for at least a decade.

The 7 Deadly Sins Of The Phone Interview

If you want to book lots of interviews for yourself, you're going to have to know what to do, and, more importantly, what not to do in that first phone interview.

The things to do are:

1 Keep your CV handy so you can discuss your experience and skills intelligently.
2 Make the best first impression you can.
3 Stay positive about yourself, the opportunity, and your desire to pursue it further.
4 Sell yourself throughout the call.
5 Only ask questions to clarify what you should discuss to sell yourself even more.
6 Tell the interviewer you are very interested in continuing with discussions. (Don't assume that she already thinks you are.)
7 Make sure you don't end the call before trying your best to book a face-to-face interview.

The Things Not To Do (aka The 7 Deadly Sins Of The Phone Interview) Are:

1 Don't ask the interviewer more questions about the job and the company than the interviewer asks you about yourself. (You aren't the one doing the interviewing at this point.)

2 Don't tell the interviewer that you already have interviews scheduled for such-and-such a day. (All that does is tell the interviewer that you aren't loyal, you aren't dedicated to their opportunity and you aren't very shrewd, if you are talking about an opportunity with a competitor.)

3 Don't dismiss an opportunity, no matter how bad a match you think it might be.

4 Don't yawn, talk to other people in the room, take another phone call, answer your mobile, or click away on your keyboard while conducting the phone interview. (All these are easy ways of showing your complete lack of professionalism.)

5 Don't go off on tangents about unrelated subjects during the call. (If the conversation isn't squarely on the topic of selling you as the best candidate for the job, you're spoiling this call.)

6 Don't let your annoying verbal tics come out during the call or during any of the interviewing process. (Let all those bad habits come forward to drive your colleagues mad after you get the job, you know what I mean? Umm, you know, umm, like, right? Umm, you know, umm, you know, right?)

7 Don't tell the interviewer you want to think about the opportunity and you will get back to him or her! (As soon as you hang up the phone, the job is gone, and so are the other possible opportunities that were waiting for you at that company!)

The 7 Deadlier Sins Of The Face-to-Face Interview

The whole point of accepting all those interviews is so you can get the practice you need to become a great interviewee. You may think that once you get your foot in the door, you can do a great job of getting the job. That may be so. But I'm certain you will find there is at least one, or maybe even a couple, of deadly sins you've been committing on a regular basis. If, like many people you hate interviews because you are uncomfortable talking about yourself and don't really have a clue about what you should and shouldn't be doing in an interview, keep reading. Everything you learn in the following pages will help you improve your game, regardless of how good or bad you are right now. Just as with phone interviews, the cardinal rule (although I'm not sure many cardinals look for work, or have a set of rules for looking for a job) for face-to-face interviewing is to treat every opportunity as if it is the best one ever!

Your attitude is a bigger deciding-factor in recruiting you than your skills and experience. That doesn't mean you can get a job without any experience or skill sets, but you could have the best combination of any candidate the company is interviewing and, if your attitude is poor, they probably won't employ you.

> 'Employers don't want to work with someone with a
> poor attitude any more than you want to work for
> a boss who's an idiot!'

A poor attitude is more than just being rude, negative, cynical, overly aggressive, or obnoxious. If you walk into the interview sounding depressed, underwhelmed by the job, or just casually interested, the interviewer is going to be motivated to get you out of the door before you bring him down and ruin his day!

When preparing for and conducting your interviews, there are some basic dos and don'ts that are very similar to the phone interview rules, but you have the added challenge of being in an unknown environment, of sitting across from the individual who is scrutinising you and of being unable to fidget while talking (the way you probably were during the phone interview. . .).

The things to do are:

1   Refer to your CV while discussing yourself. (Bring a copy for yourself, as well as some spares, in case you need to hand them out to additional people you speak to in the course of the interview(s).)
2   Be prepared to discuss yourself in detail. (Don't rely on the interviewer to ask you the right questions; that doesn't always happen.)
3   Have a good idea of what the job entails before you walk into the interview and have a list of your experiences and skills that cover those job activities. (Be prepared to direct the conversation so that it

covers each one of these points. You have a better understanding of what the job entails than the interviewer does, so you'll have to feed him or her the questions. Try to make the interviewer think he or she is brilliant for asking you about your experience with so-and-so and how that makes you perfectly qualified to deal with it at his or her company.)

4   Keep track of every one of the skills you have covered in the interview. (Your goal is to have covered every one of them before you leave the interview. If you don't, you won't have done your best to sell yourself!)

5   Be prepared for some of the standard, poor interview questions such as 'So, tell me about yourself', 'Give me a couple of examples where you had a difficult situation and how you overcame it' or 'Where do you see yourself in five years time?' These are all lousy interviewer questions; interviewers ask them because they don't have a clue what questions to ask to work out if you are a good candidate. (But beware: you could easily go down the wrong path with these inane questions. So don't use them as a chance to share your frustrations about your last job, boss or personal issues!)

6   Don't lose your energy or enthusiasm as the day wears on. You may have to talk to other people after the main interview – either formally or informally. Stamina is also required for second or third round interviews. Remember you have to answer all the questions enthusiastically, however many times you've been asked them! All the people you speak to will have some input into the decision-making process, and, if you put even one of them off, you could seriously affect the result!

7   Bring a notepad and a pen to the interviews. Take notes. It makes you look very interested in the opportunity and it's a huge compliment to the interviewer. (And you can refer back to your notes later when you write your post-interview thank-you letter.)

The things not to do (the 7 deadlier sins of the face-to-face interview) are:

1   Don't turn your first face-to-face interview into an interview about the company. (If your agenda for walking into the

interview is to determine if this is a job in a company that you want, then it obviously isn't your agenda to get a job. I've said it before and I'll say it again: You don't know where your next great opportunity will come from and, if you start dismissing jobs because you know you're too good for them, you are driving right past all of the hidden opportunities you conducted this campaign to find.)

2   Don't ever, under any circumstances, for any reason, at all, ever bad mouth your former employer, colleagues, past experiences, or talk politics. (Unless your goal is to demonstrate you will be a valuable addition to the company's gossip committee, bringing your own brand of bad workplace attitude to the masses.)

3   Don't bring a mobile to the interview. (If you have a call that's more important than landing your next job, stay at home and let that pay the bills.)

4   Don't forget personal hygiene.

5   Don't be late. (Keeping your potential boss sitting there waiting only gives him or her more time to imagine what it will be like to watch you saunter into the office 20 minutes late every day.)

6   Don't give the interviewer an ultimatum. (By telling them that you need a decision before you leave, you are really telling them that you're an idiot. They would assume that as a professional, you would understand that they need to evaluate you just as much as you would want to evaluate them.)

7   Don't be the first one to bring up salary. (You have the advantage. If you used my suggestion for the covering letter, you have already told the interviewer how much money you need, and he called you knowing your expectations in advance. It's likely that he either has a budget that matches what you want, or he thinks he can make an offer that is likely to tempt you.)

Never Walk Out Of The Door Without Knowing Where You Stand In The Running

Never leave an interview without knowing if you are still being considered for the job. How are you going to follow up and re-sell yourself effectively if you don't know what's putting them off you?

It's really just as simple as asking:

- Where do I stand in the process?
- Do you think I would make a good candidate?
- Are there any relevant strengths I didn't fully explain?
- If you were to make a call tomorrow for second round interviews, would I be one of them?

If the interviewer tells you that he was very impressed, great! Ask when you can expect a follow-up call, and if there is anything you can do in the meantime to help the decision-making process. If he tells you something that leads you to believe you didn't do well (like saying that he doesn't think you're a good fit for the position), ask what areas he thinks you fall short on, and don't try to argue with him about it. Lead him to believe that you are just trying to determine where you should be applying yourself in future job applications. In reality you are going to use this information in your thank-you letter, when you try to do some damage control. (Remember the sample letters in Chapter 5?) Know where you stand in the running before you leave so you know the next step in handling this opportunity: damage control or more selling.

Whether or not you are a definite for the job or the least likely person in the world to get the position, your next step is to send a thank-you letter for his time, so that you can once again re-sell yourself for that job!

A Good Example Of What Not To Do When The Calls Start Coming In

One of the worst nightmares of my career working with job-seekers occurred relatively early on. It hasn't happened since, because I've never forgotten to warn my clients about it.

One of my first clients, Tony T., was a loud, cocky, stockbroker. He had worked his way up to a nice position with one of the largest financial firms in the world, but downsizing can catch up with anyone, so out he went.

We did a lot of work together. He was difficult to work with because his communication skills were very poor. As difficult as it was, he had a great CV because he had been very successful. On paper, he was a real catch.

On paper.

The fact that he was a pain in the neck is not the reason I remember Tony. The reason I remember him is because he made one of the worst mistakes in the business. He made a potential employer feel as if they weren't his first choice to work for. Tony didn't tell the callers that he wasn't interested in working for them – quite the opposite, in fact. In his loud and abrasive way, he thought he was selling to them how interested in the job he was. But what he was actually doing was answering questions without thinking first.

When the recruiting manager called him and started asking questions, Tony didn't have anything prepared. He was a seasoned professional, after all, and speaking off the cuff was nothing new for him. So, when each of the callers asked him the innocuous question 'How did you hear about us?' he replied by saying that he 'paid a company to post his CV to 3,000 companies, and you must have been one of them'.

And when they asked him why he thought he would be a good candidate for the job, he replied by saying, 'Didn't you read my CV? I paid a lot of money for that thing, and there's loads of info in there'.

'Be prepared, and always THINK before you speak!'

Needless to say, he didn't get any job offers. In fact, out of the more than 10 calls he got, only one ever called him back, and he only made it to the first round of face-to-face interviews.

Never make a company feel that they're your second choice. If you don't come across as being in love with the company and the opportunity they are presenting to you, why should the company fall in love with you? When you are faced with the question of 'how did you hear about us?' always be honest, but in a tactful way. What Tony should have said (and you should, too) is that he did some research on the internet and, through his network, found their company. He was impressed with their work and felt he could make a valuable contribution. He should have then said he was flattered that they approached him and that he was excited to learn more about the opportunity. When you turn the conversation back to them, the interviewer will usually drop the difficult subject because people love to talk about themselves.

Also, never tell the interviewer that an answer to the question is on your CV. I can't tell you how many times I interview clients and when I ask them a question related to their background and experience, they tell me that it's on their CV. Your job is to answer questions and put the most impressive sales spin possible on those answers. Your job is not to be a lazy, unprepared slob, hoping that your CV will do your work for you. If you can't communicate your successes in a conversation, it's very likely that the interviewer will assume that it's because you aren't really successful.

Keep Your Expectations Realistic

Don't count your chickens before they hatch and, more importantly, don't crush any eggs before you know what's in them! It's vital that you set your expectations before you conduct your job search. My friends are always amazed I don't get at all upset when I get bad service and terrible food when we eat at the local greasy spoon, but I'm quick to call the waiter if my steak isn't cooked the way I like it at a nice restaurant. I explain to them that it's because I set my expectations accordingly. When I go to a dingy corner cafe or a fast food place, I don't expect to have good service, and I definitely don't expect the food to be five-star. You don't get a complete meal, with salad, soup, and pudding, for ten quid and expect quality to be included. But you do expect a quality meal, with quick and courteous service if you're paying £40, a la carte!

My client, Frank, is a perfect example of not setting expectations appropriately before a job search. When we started the campaign, during the mailing list consultation process, one of the main things we discussed was his preferred geographical area. Some people love to travel, and relocating every couple of years is part of the excitement of life, whereas others have roots that go deep, and moving just isn't an option. I understand that and respect it.

Frank wanted to conduct his search on a national level, so that's just what we did. He was looking for a logistics coordinator job, a nice middle-of-the-road position, so there were lots of companies that were a good fit for him. When we posted his CV to the top 1,000 of them, needless to say, Frank got great results. Within a week he told me that he had received more than two dozen calls – two dozen calls from potential employers that were quite impressed with his CV and would love to talk about a job with him! But when Frank told me about his results, he wasn't happy. Just the opposite: he was very upset, telling me that he hadn't got a single good lead! I was of course completely confused, he just said he had got more than 20 calls from companies that wanted to discuss jobs with him, yet here he was shouting at me for letting him down. I was confused.

When I finally calmed him down and managed to get him to explain himself, he told me that, though he had had all those calls, as soon as he asked the caller if relocation was necessary, and they said possibly, he immediately said no thanks and got off the phone.

I was shocked. Not only did he fail to set his expectations correctly during the planning stage, but he also failed to tell me what his real desires were. And he also threw away perfect opportunities to negotiate for a virtual-office or non-relocation position!

Never turn down, or even discount, a potential employer before you have approached, sought out an opportunity, and then proven yourself as the candidate of choice. At that point, if there are special provisions or caveats, you can negotiate them.

> 'Nobody will entertain your special needs before they've decided they like you.'

The first thing to do when looking for work is to set your expectations correctly and never let special circumstances interfere with you selling yourself 100%, *before* you bring up your special requests.

✓ Your Days 7–9 Assignment

Step 1

Book appointments. Lots of appointments. Have your CV and the list of the companies that you've posted your CV to handy. Stay positive and sell yourself in every call. Practise overcoming difficult questions like why you're looking for work and whether you have degree in such-and-such.

Step 2

Practise selling yourself on the phone and in person. Know what your strengths and weaknesses are, and be ready to sell the strengths while overcoming the problem areas. Never let an opportunity pass you by. Never forget that you don't know where your next great job is; it might be hidden behind a boring-sounding first call!

Step 3

Go to as many interviews as you can. Take an outline about yourself (in addition to your CV) to every interview. Create a job description of the position you're being interviewed for and a list of the skills and experiences you have that make you the best candidate for the job. Make sure you have extra copies of your CV to hand out. (They beat a business card every time!) Take a prepared list of topics to discuss, with good examples of your previous work experience to show how you've overcome problems and challenges in the past.

7. Day 10

Accepting Several Job Offers!

Don't Just Take The First Thing That Comes Along – Take Everything That Comes Along

I have heard everyone, from know-nothings to career industry experts, say it is wrong, or immoral, or dishonest for a job-seeker to accept more than one offer. Their argument for not doing so is that it will cost that employer thousands of pounds to look for another candidate and, in the meantime, they still won't have someone for the job.

What they fail to mention is that employers do exactly the same thing to job-seekers every day! How immoral is that? How much does it cost the real, breathing, family-supporting person they just did that to? I have a lot less trouble sleeping at night if a major company spends £2,000 to find a good candidate, only to lose that employee at the 11th hour, than if my client 'spends' £2,000 in lost income being strung along with the 'we are going to be making a decision in another two weeks' or 'the Director is on holiday until next Friday' rubbish.

If you're being given one of those lines, or something similar, I have a very unpleasant reality check for you: they have already recruited someone else, and they are keeping you in reserve in case he doesn't show up or work out! Horrible, but true. (And if you hear this from a recruitment consultant, he didn't have an opportunity for you in the first place; he just wanted to keep you out of the hands of a competing recruiter, on the off chance that he does find an opportunity to sell you to a company. Remember that recruiters aren't free. They charge your future employer a sales commission when they place you. That commission can run from as little as a few hundred pounds to a percentage of your first year's salary! That's a shedload of money to hire you!)

> 'Companies are keeping you on the back burner in case the other person doesn't turn up!'

So, when someone tells you that you are hurting a company, remember what they will do and have done to you. Don't hate companies for doing this to you; just be aware that they do it. Remember: most companies aren't run by people. They are controlled by platoons of heartless corporate money men, looking at nothing but the bottom line, regardless of who or what falls by the wayside in the quest for an additional $1/4\%$ in annual earnings.

The reason I'm suggesting that you accept more than one offer, or seriously pursue/entertain more than one offer, is not to 'stick it to the man'. I'm telling you to do this so that you can put yourself into the driver's seat in your job search. If you only have one opportunity in front of you, you are being driven by that offer. You have nothing to compare it to. (Comparing it to jobs that you would like to have is the same as comparing this job offer to, 'What if I won the National Lottery?') You are limited in your options and have little or no leverage to make this a better opportunity. You could lie and pretend that you are currently reviewing several other great opportunities, but in the end you will still be under a lot of pressure to make this opportunity count because you have nothing else.

If they haven't made an offer, you don't have anything. It's just another prospect. It's great to have lots of prospects, but they don't count when you're analysing offers.

> 'Opportunities are NOT the same as offers. So don't count your jobs before they're offered!'

On the other hand, when you have more than one offer you have manoeuvred yourself into the driver's seat. Now you can use your situation to your advantage. You really can tell them that you have other offers that you're reviewing. You can also play one against the other, improving each offer until you have the BEST VALUE you can possibly get from each one.

Leverage: Making The Offers Even Better!

Leverage is when you have a greater advantage than the opposing force. In this case, you go from a situation of being in a buyer's market (employers have the advantage in this day and age, with so many job-seekers out there looking for work, through no fault of their own, and with so many ways of making themselves known) to a seller's market.

This is when you aren't desperate to become employed, you don't have just one opportunity staring at you, and your confidence level rises. Confidence comes through loud and clear to your potential employers. Don't worry; you won't scare them off. They LOVE confidence. (But don't be an arrogant idiot, acting as if you're a celebrity and thinking you can get whatever you want. They like you, but they don't *really* like you.)

Your confidence will enable you to look more objectively at the jobs placed before you and make counteroffers, if appropriate. You will have the luxury of being able to decide if this job will have the career path that you really want, or if this other offer gives you more cash in your pocket in a shorter amount of time than the others.

Doesn't that scenario sound better than secretly thinking to yourself that, if you don't take this job, the house is going to get repossessed, or you can get used to making x% less money, just eat baked beans, and never go out ever again?

My client, Jennifer (who I talked about in an earlier chapter), is a great example of accepting multiple job offers. Jennifer is an extreme example of the leverage scenario. She is a bright young woman with excellent skills for just above a starting role. She also had a great opportunity to maximise her earning potential. If she had taken the first job she was offered, or turned down all but the last one, she would not be the Assistant Director at one of the largest employers in her town, only a year after finishing university. In fact, she might very well have ended up with a low-level job making less money than she deserved, simply because she had no leverage and took the first thing that came along. Instead, she accepted all of the offers, made them wait long enough to complete her interviews, and then laid all of the opportunities out in front of her and objectively looked at each one, weighing up the pros and cons for each.

Another way to accomplish this, without actually accepting the offer, is to push it out for a short time, by asking for a few days to review the offer. Once you have accumulated a few offers, you can then review each position, looking at its good and bad merits, just as Jenny did. The advantage you have in this process is that you can then go back to each of those employers and continue to make the most of your situation. You can now play one offer against another, nudging the good ones up to make them great!

Using One Offer To Improve Another Offer

Take care, as this is a power tool. As is the case with any power tool, there is a risk of accidents if you're not careful! Make sure you read, understand, and follow all the safety rules in your owner's manual before operation.

Counteroffers: make one and the first offer is off the table. (So be sure you aren't bluffing yourself into an 'all-in' loser hand.) If you aren't happy with the offer a company has made, by all means, consider making a counteroffer, but be sure that you aren't pricing yourself out of the job. Sometimes, the reality is they can't afford you. The standard rule of thumb in negotiating is that, if you make a counterproposal, the company is no longer obliged to keep to the first offer. This means that they have the option to either accept your counterproposal, stand firm and stay with their first offer, or tell you, 'No deal, we're going with someone else'.

Be tactful when making a counteroffer. Don't tell them so-and-so (The Competitor) offered you seven grand more, and they either improve on that or you'll take your talents to the other team! Nobody likes ultimatums, especially potential employers. It's highly unlikely that they will be contacting you with a new offer.

Instead, explain to Company A that you are quite excited about the job, but you have been in an aggressive job search and there is another company that has made an offer as well. Tell them you are thinking very seriously about the offer that Company A has made, but Company B is also including an employee benefits package that is really attractive to you (or is also including a year-end bonus that would put you closer to your desired total salary range) than what Company A has offered. Tell Company A that you would really like to discuss the opportunity further, but is there any way to get the pay package more in line with Company B? (Of course, you always want to get an offer in writing before you make a counteroffer. That way you can respond to it point by point in your argument.)

The other benefit of having more than one job offer to pit against another is the intangible benefits. Finding a job that pays well is great, but there are other factors that can make a great-paying job a poor choice. When you have several options available, the other factors to consider become the ones that will ultimately dictate whether you learn to love, or hate, your new job.

> 'Money, career path and happiness are the true benchmarks of a successful job search.'

The hidden benefits of the job are the things that you can't negotiate into a counteroffer – things like location. Will you have to drive an hour in traffic jams twice a day, or is it less than a mile from your house? You should also consider your new colleagues. It would be great if you could tell your future boss that you'll take the job, but only if he gives the boot to that annoying woman who'll be sitting opposite you. Just walking down the corridor was enough to tell you that she'll be the main reason you'll be looking for work again in three months! The other intangibles to consider are the responsibilities of the new job. Are they in line with your career path? Will the responsibilities go beyond the pay? (How many times have you known someone – including yourself – who was in a job where he or she worked more hours, did more tasks, and took more trouble than the pay justified?).

What about the career path? If you take the job, will there be a defined path for you at the company? (Waiting for your boss to die so you can get promoted does not count as a career path!) Does this company offer the flexibility you need? Do your kids have lots of after-school activities? Does one of the opportunities you're looking at require you to work late at least twice a week? Do they offer the option of working from home on occasion? Do they have a decent leave scheme (paid time off, flexitime and so on) that will allow you to go to doctors' appointments and get domestic and personal stuff sorted from time to time?

Having multiple job offers to play off against each other gives you the chance to not only find the job that offers the most money and best benefits, but it also enables you to find the job that will provide you with the highest level of happiness. Finding the best balance of those things is the real benchmark of a successful job search campaign. The only sure way to maximise all of the elements of the great job you're looking for is to have multiple job offers to choose from!

✓ Your Day 10 Assignment

Step 1

Make a list of the key elements that will make a great new job for you. List them in order of preference. If money is the most important, put it at the top of the list. If location or job title get you more excited than the money, that's fine, too. Just be honest with yourself when you're making the list. Once the offers come in, this is what you are going to be grading them against, so, if you're not being honest, you'll only let yourself down in the long run.

Step 2

Create a game plan for collecting job offers. Depending on your level on the corporate ladder, it might make more sense to accept offers outright and just push back the start date, or ask for evaluation time. Do you plan to make counteroffers? (And if so, why?) Don't think that you should make a counteroffer regardless of their first offer. Sometimes, the first offer is the best offer. However, leaving room to negotiate is never a bad option. Either way you choose to go, have a plan in place before you go to the interviews. Keep your reason for asking for more time to consider the offer consistent; it means you won't have to worry about what you said to whom.

Step 3

Evaluate the offers with your family, your significant other, your best friend, your mentor, the neighbour – anyone! You have to bring someone else in to add the objectivity that you lack. This is the last step in a hard process; you've spent a considerable amount of time, effort, and, probably, money to get to this point. Don't slow down now. Reviewing the pros and cons of job offers is harder than you think. Sometimes you might be won over by the sales pitch that a company has made. (Trust me: they all make a sales pitch. Some companies go so far as to use the same tricks and techniques of a good timeshare swindle to lure good candidates onto the team!) If you let your emotions rule over the facts, you may soon regret your decision. The best way to avoid this is to include someone else in the evaluation process.

Make it someone you know and someone who has an idea of what makes you tick, but who will also look logically at the offers before you and can help you weigh up your options intelligently. Ultimately, the decision is yours, but you will be much more confident in your decision if you've thought it through with someone else.

8. Negotiating the Best Possible Salary

If you've never negotiated for your salary before, this can be an intimidating idea. Quite often, clients tell me that they can't negotiate for a better salary because (pick the one(s) that you think apply to you, too) they are in a bad economy; their industry is too tight; they don't make lots of money the way executives who normally 'negotiate' their salary do; they don't have the skills to negotiate; they don't even know what they're worth, let alone what's the most a company would be willing to pay them; and/or they're afraid to negotiate because they might lose the job offer. I know you probably fall into at least one, more likely two, three, or more of these categories. First let me just tell you, YOU ARE WRONG. Let's break down these excuses and take an honest look at each of them.

- *Economy* If a poor economy was a valid excuse here, the company wouldn't be interviewing you; they would be shutting the doors and hiding cash under their mattresses. Nine times out of 10, when prospects or clients tell me they aren't getting job offers because the economy is bad, what they subconsciously mean is that they have a poor CV, they haven't been doing much at all to get it in front of the right people, and their results have been dismal. OK, they could be honest with themselves and admit that they're not great at looking for jobs, but that wouldn't be nearly as easy, or guilt-free, as just blaming the economy.

- *Industry* Every industry goes through its ups and downs. They are all cyclical in nature. Telecom booms, then it busts. It's the same for manufacturing, and retail and technology . . . all of them. However, if you have got to the point where a company is entering into salary negotiations with you, then your industry obviously isn't doing too badly. Regardless of the status of an industry, recruiting managers are always interested in adding high quality individuals to their team.

■ *Not an Executive* When I talk to people who only make £20,000 or £30,000 a year, and they tell me they don't earn enough to justify negotiating, I want to wring their necks! The lower you are on the corporate ladder, the less money you earn, the easier it is to negotiate! Think about it. If you're currently making £10 an hour, and you've just received an offer of £12 an hour, you are probably happy, aren't you? (After all, that's a 20% increase in pay!) Now, if you go back and negotiate for a little more money, you may only add another 50p or £1 an hour – and that's small change for most companies – but for you, that's another 5 to 10% increase in income!

■ *No Skills* You may think you don't have any negotiating skills but, again, you're wrong. We all negotiate, all the time. Children are natural negotiators. How many times have your children come to you with a request that they knew was totally outrageous, but they made a convincing enough argument to persuade you to go for it? And how many times did you negotiate with them in return for that request? It's human nature to negotiate. The trick is to understand what you want, and then have a good technique to get it.

■ *Don't Know Your Worth* This is probably the most common issue I come across. People just don't know what they are worth in the marketplace. It's a real shame when you consider how easy the information is to get. In less than 60 seconds on Google, I found more than 370,000 individual results for salary information, and 29,900 for salary calculators! You must be really afraid of finding out what you're worth if you honestly don't think there is any way to work out what you're worth.

■ *Fear* This is probably the most legitimate excuse of the whole lot. This one I can believe. Fear is the number one reason people avoid negotiating for a better salary. Fear of the unknown. Fear of rejection. Fear of ruining it and getting less than they originally offered. Fear of losing the opportunity all together. Fear of the unknown and fear of rejection are legitimate concerns. Neither one can really hurt you; they are both artificial fears, because the unknown is never as bad as you think it is, and rejection happens to you every day. Usually you don't even notice it, so creating a phobia of going for the things you want, based on a fear of something that you deal with every day, is just plain daft.

The last two fears are completely unreal. Getting less money than the original offer is just not going to happen. The worst that can happen is that they don't go for the higher salary and you have to either accept the offer at the original number or walk away.

What about fear of losing the opportunity altogether? Well, if you've made it this far in the process, and a company has made you an offer, they're obviously very interested in you. If you ask for more money, they might say no, but it is very highly unlikely that they will tell you to get lost. If anything, your new boss will have a higher level of respect for you because you have clearly demonstrated that you believe you are worth more.

Don't Undervalue Yourself (But Don't Price Yourself Out Of The Running)

When approaching companies and, later, during the negotiation phase, it is critical that your salary expectations match your market value. If your job title, in your local geography, merits an average income of, say, £25,000 on the low end, to £36,000 on the high end, your expectations should be within that range. If you have little to no experience, common sense would tell you that you probably fall closer to the low end than the high, but that doesn't mean you have to expect the lowest available salary! If for some reason you believe you should be earning significantly more than the average range, you should either have an incredibly good reason (and one that you can explain and justify convincingly to a future employer) or you should re-evaluate your goals. Maybe you are expecting more money than you might be entitled to at this point in your career or, more likely, you aren't in the right job to earn what you want. If that's the case, you should sit down and determine what would be the right field and job type for you to begin earning the money you want. If you're looking to double your income and your industry and job level don't warrant an increase of that magnitude, it's very likely that negotiating an offer won't get you where you want to be.

Outrageous expectations aside, there are two other issues to be aware of when you are pricing yourself: asking for too much and asking for too little. Believe it or not, you will probably generate far fewer responses by asking for too little money than by asking for more!

When you ask for too much money, there's a very big chance that you will price yourself right out of the running. However, some managers will see what you have to offer and will still want to call you in, knowing that they could talk you down and get you for far less than you are asking. The other risk when asking for too much money is that you will often find yourself being labelled 'overqualified' – i.e. 'too expensive!' However, when you ask for too little money, you wave a red flag that says, 'Look out – I'm damaged goods!'

Think about it. You're looking around a car showroom and you see a very nice car. When you ask the salesman how much, if he replies with a number that is a little higher than you are expecting, you won't be shocked, but you'll think, 'If I want this car, I'll have to do some haggling. I'll start by offering him half his asking price'.

If, on the other hand, the salesman tells you the car is only £350, you'll do a double take and immediately start inspecting it more closely, trying to find the flood damage, the crumpled frame, and/or the missing engine parts. If something seems too good to be true, it probably is.

How To Work Out What You're Worth

Working out your value is quite easy in the age of the internet. The main variables when it comes to determining what you are worth are the work and the geography. If you are the managing director (MD) of a medium-sized service company, you might very well command a solid six figure salary in Edinburgh or London. But that same level of responsibility in a small town in, for example, the Lancashire countryside will earn you less. Of course, the cost of living plays a huge role in salary ranges. If an MD were to live in Edinburgh, his three-bedroom, two-bathroom house would cost him around £400,000. Now, say that same great MD decided to live in a nice little town in Lancashire, he could get the same house for much less. His other expenses would be less as well, so his meagre salary would take him just as far as the big city MD's hefty salary. Earning £70,000 might sound nice, but if you're doing it in London, where an average meal might cost you £50 a person, and you're spending more than £300 a month on taxis, plus £500 or more a month for car payments, insurance, and parking, that seventy grand starts to look smaller and smaller by the minute!

It's important that you know what you're worth before you enter the job market. Also understand the cost of living. This is especially true if your goal is to relocate. I can't tell you how many times I have spoken to people who decide to relocate permanently from the 'big city' and expect to find a job making the same money. It usually comes as a big shock to them that they are no longer going to make £300,000 a year as an assistant director of a bank, or whatever it is that they did before. Houses are cheaper, taxes are cheaper, food is cheaper and companies are cheaper! That oversight on their part usually equates to several months of fruitless job searching before they get an 'attitude update' and realise it really does cost more to live in paradise – it's just that the expense comes from lower wages, not higher prices!

The best way for you to work out what you should be making, based on your level of experience, industry, and geography, is to use a salary calculator. You can try WorkSmart (www.worksmart.org.uk). You can also get details of salary ranges for specific jobs through Prospects, the graduate careers website at www.prospects.ac.uk. There are also lots of dedicated salary checker websites (provided by recruitment consultancies) scattered across the internet. Do an internet search and try a few. But make sure you know your worth before you start negotiating your salary.

How To Avoid Going For Jobs That Don't Pay Enough

In Chapter 2 I advised you to include your salary requirements in your covering letter, and now I'm going to tell you not to be the first one to discuss money. It seems contradictory, but it isn't. Even though you have mentioned money in your covering letter, you still haven't discussed it with the employer. Every piece of advice I'm giving you is the same, whether you put your compensation in the letter or not. Never be the first one to talk about money. The reason I include money in my clients' covering letters is so that they only receive calls for reasonably qualified opportunities. By that I mean that the caller has an understanding of what range of money the job-seeker is looking for and has made the decision that he or she still wants to approach the seeker, whether he or she can offer him that amount or not.

Of course, as I explained in Chapter 2, when you present the salary requirements as a range, you are opening yourself up to a greater range of variables than just what you put on paper. The employer can look at your recent salary history and decide to try to recruit you on the low end of what you want, perhaps by offering add-on incentives in the form of performance bonuses, and so forth. Or the employer may have a budget that is even higher than what you asked for, and he knows that if he really wants you, he can make an offer that is at, or higher than, your high-end, and he can be fairly sure you will be motivated to take the offer.

So, if you do include your salary goals in the covering letter, it's likely that the person you are talking to has already decided that he or she can come to an agreement with you that would meet your needs.

On the other hand, by including your salary desires in writing, you are committing yourself (in a very loose way) to a range of compensation. That isn't necessarily a bad thing in and of itself, especially if the comp range you included is within the scope of what you genuinely feel you deserve, and would be happy with. However, there are people out there, the ones who consider themselves to be talented salespeople, who would rather not limit their earning requirements and who feel comfortable with the fact that, by leaving the money out of the covering letter, will be more likely to be contacted by employers who would love to recruit them, but couldn't even begin to pay them what they want. These are the individuals who love to sell. They usually think that if they can get their foot in the door and meet face to face with a recruitment manager, they can convince that person that they are not only worth the money that they'll ask for, but they also believe that they have a reasonable chance of negotiating a way for the employers to afford them.

I say good for you, if that's your attitude. One of the main reasons successful salespeople are so successful is because they are completely barmy. They love negotiating, and there is no challenge too big for them! I would rather know that I'm not wasting my time on an opportunity that turns out to be for a job that can only afford to pay me half what I need. In my own job search I would include the salary, but in plenty of my clients' job searches I leave out the compensation. This is really a personal choice, and there are as many pros as there are cons for each, so I will let you decide.

Getting Sign-on Bonuses And Relocation Reimbursements: Make Them Bribe You!

'Always negotiate face to face or, at the very least, on the phone. Never try to negotiate by email!'

If a company wants you badly enough but can't meet your salary demands, they might try to sway you by offering you a sign-on bonus. Signing bonuses are a one-time payment that isn't included in your base salary (on which everything else is calculated). It's really a good-faith demonstration that the company agrees you're worth more than the job pays, but they can't justify it to the money men. In effect, they are bribing you to come to work for them! (Caution: You might have to sign a contract committing to a period of time on the job and, if you don't stay for that length of time, you have to pay the bonus back!)

The best way to work out how much a sign-on bonus should be is to think about the expenses you'll incur for changing employers – like relocation and cost-of-living difference, as well as the base salary, how demanding the role is, and how hard it is for a company to fill the role.

The major factor in commanding a really big bonus (I'm talking about something above and beyond payment to cover relocation etc.) is if the position is either a high-profile one, or if you are already doing the same thing for one of their competitors. (Companies like benefiting at the expense of the competition!)

Hidden sign-on bonuses include holiday time, extra time off (paid or unpaid), insurance plans, subsidised childcare, a company gym, flexible hours with telecommuting, and unpaid work breaks. Not every bonus is a cash bonus. Not all non-cash bonuses are truly non-cash! If you could negotiate an extra week's holiday a year, how much would that be worth to you in cash? Probably more than the 40 hours' pay? If you have other commitments in your life that require some flexibility, negotiating time off from work or the option of taking work home with you into your compensation package is of greater value than a one-off payment could ever be. (It's the bonus that keeps on giving!) These are all things to consider when taking on a job offer, especially if the offer is below what you were hoping for (and after you have made it clear to the recruitment manager that he or she is offering you less than you think you are worth). Extra holiday time, flexible hours, and variable insurance benefits are the things that they can get in under the radar of the company money men!

Getting All The Commitments In Writing (An Insurance Policy For Your New Job)

Before negotiating, whether it's for the salary and benefits or the job itself, make sure you get everything in writing! I can't tell you how many times my clients have been let down by their last employers. They were promised one set of responsibilities and expectations during the 'dating' phase of the job, and, once they were 'married', everything changed! (Two words of advice for any single readers: pre-nuptial agreement.)

Quite often, a company will paint a rosy picture about the condition of things in an effort to tempt you. They want you to work there, they know there are aspects of the job that aren't great and their plan is that, once they have you on the team, they can and will drop all that on you. Don't let it happen! Get EVERYTHING in writing: the base salary; the insurance; and profit sharing, when it starts, and how much. Also, include the things you might not think of are important now, but that you'll be thankful for later on when they try to say they employed you to do them (things such as the detailed duties of the job). What are your quotas and goals? What are your measurable indices and what is the agreed-upon value for success?

A warning before you run off and ask for that sign-on bonus you deserve: When you negotiate for a sign-on bonus, you are getting a one-off bonus. You will always benefit more by getting more money in your salary, as it will have repercussions year after year. (If you get that £3,500 bonus, you only get paid once. If, on the other hand, you manage to get that £3,500 added to your base salary, you'll get it again next year – and when you get your annual pay rise, the percentage is calculated on that higher base!)

The Numbers Game

Any company you approach will know what you are worth before you turn up. When you enter an interview, the interviewer has a number in mind for what he or she is willing to pay you, based on what other people in your industry and geography, are getting. You should, too!

'You can't really negotiate until the number is on the table.'

The first step in making sure you come out of the salary negotiations in one piece is to have a minimum salary figure already in your head before you walk in through the door. And whatever you do, don't tell them what it is! You are now playing a numbers game, and the first person to blink loses. Your goal is to get them to commit to a number before you do!

One of the tricks to be aware of before you get started: Companies ask you how much you want. They often go as far as putting the harmless-sounding 'desired salary range' on their application forms. We are trained from birth to fill in all the blanks, so we do. Bad idea.

If a company makes an offer and it is better than your minimum salary number, take it! If, on the other hand, they make an offer that is too low, tell them it's too low. But don't say by how much! Say it's too low, not that it's £8,500 too little. Don't do it!

If the interviewer asks you how much money you want, reply like this: 'I'm really more interested in doing (this type of work) with your company, than I am in the INITIAL offer size.' Learn this response off by heart! It tells the interviewer that you are more interested in the job than the salary (even if it's not really the case) and immediately differentiates you from the money-grabbing masses that have come before you! Plus, you avoided their question. That's brilliant! If that doesn't call their bluff, and they ask you the money question again, answer with this: 'I'll CONSIDER any REASONABLE offer.' Talk about the perfect politician's nothing-said answer! 'Consider' gives you lots of room to manoeuvre, and 'reasonable' is nice and vague! The ball is back in their court. You've been very tactful, yet managed to say nothing. Any politician would be proud of you.

By now, quite often, you've won the game, and they've made an offer, which is great. However, it isn't that uncommon for the interviewer to play hardball, coming back again with the same question, perhaps worded slightly differently. If he does, it's time to pull out the classic line, 'You're in a much better position to know what I'm worth to you than I am.' There you go! You were nice, but you just told him that you're onto his game, and you aren't going for it. Repeat this last step as often as necessary until he finally gets the hint and makes an offer.

OK vs. Hmmm

This is a trick that I learned from a client many years ago. He learned it from his grandfather, who used to be a car trader. (I later found the same technique in a great book titled *Negotiating Your Salary: How to Make $1000 a Minute* by Jack Chapman.) Whether my client learned it from his grandfather or not, I don't know, but it certainly isn't rocket science, and we have all done it subconsciously a million times. Anything that comes so naturally to all of us, has to be good!

Basically it works this way: if someone makes you an offer, don't reply with a yes, even if it's light years beyond your wildest expectations. The last thing you want to do is sound excited. It undermines your negotiating power and, ultimately, the manager or seller feels terrible about the situation. (More about that in a minute.) Instead, when they make an offer, say, 'Hmmm'. Or better yet, if they give you a salary number or range, repeat the number or the higher end of the range, and THEN say 'Hmmm'. After a moment of reflection, add, 'Isn't that a little low?' or '£Blah an hour – is that the best you can do?' If it's not the best they can do, they're very likely to come back to you with a better number, and even if they say yes, that is the best they can do, you'll still have room to negotiate, and in the long run the manager will feel better about his offer.

Let me explain briefly what I mean when I say that he will feel better about his offer. Imagine that you are selling a car like my client's grandfather did. If a prospective buyer asked you how much you want for that car, and you told the buyer that you wanted a £800 for it, would you feel good if he immediately grinned and yelled, 'SOLD!'? No. You would instantly think to yourself, 'I didn't ask for enough money! I blew it, and he's stealing that old worn-out car from me!' Now, on the other hand, if, after you told him that you wanted a thousand dollars, he said to you, 'Hmmm. A thousand dollars – is that really the best you can do?' You could tell him yes, that you did the research and that's the fair market value. If he then agreed to the price; you'd feel that you did a good job and that you got a reasonable sum for the old banger.

The same principle is true for salary negotiations. Remember: It's just as important that the people on the other side of the table feel that they got a good deal, too. If they feel robbed after you walk out the door, it won't be too long before they start to really scrutinise you, looking for a way to knock you down a peg, or get you out of there and find someone else who is more reasonably priced.

The Three Cs To Consider Before You Negotiate

Before you charge through the door ready to start demanding what you're worth, take a minute to look at the big picture. While you are a great catch and you will undoubtedly bring amazing energy, insight, experience and leadership to a company, there are still a couple of other factors that come into the equation. Take a gander at those before you make your play; that way you'll be less likely to stumble two-thirds of the way through your manoeuvre!

Industry Conditions

Economy

How's the economy right now? Remember that the majority of the world operates under the 'react first' philosophy of business. If the market tilts for a microsecond, obviously the sky is falling, so let's panic first and ask questions later! Are there any market trends that would directly affect your industry? If there are, your bargaining power will be affected by it, but not at all hampered. (In fact, you would be failing in your efforts if you didn't point the trend out as a selling point in favour of recruiting you: 'Though the market is in a slump for widget sales, my track record of developing new channels is exactly what Company A needs to diversify and grow the business beyond its current shortfalls.')

> 'If you say something that isn't selling you aggressively, you should shut your mouth.'

Every word that comes out of your mouth should shout out about your talents and motivate the listener to fall deeper and more madly in love with you. If you see something that seems to be a negative about yourself, your environment or your abilities, sit down and work on a way to turn it round. There is no problem that can't be turned around to benefit you. (If there were, we wouldn't have politicians!)

Unemployment

Have there been recent redundancies in your town or your industry, creating more competition for you? If so, be aware that you will be competing with them. Get to know them. According to the *Art of War*, the best way to defeat your enemy is to know your enemy (or something like that . . .). Make every effort to find out who else the company is talking to, and then play up your strengths, while pointing out that, undoubtedly, the other candidates might be qualified,

but certainly not as much as you, nor do they have the energy and
enthusiasm for the job that you have!

Demand and difficulty

How difficult is the job? Is it a tough industry in general? The more
profession-specific the role, the more difficult it becomes for a
company to find someone who can do it, and the more valuable you
become! Do you have qualifications or degrees that make you more
attractive to an organisation? These are all things that add to your
leveraging strengths. Make a list of all of the strengths, qualifications,
experiences and abilities that make you valuable, and be prepared to
bring them up frequently during the negotiations.

Company conditions

Status. Is the company currently in profit? Are they in the red?
Is this a start-up? (If so, they need experienced people like you.)
Is the company going through a period of growth? (If they are,
they'll need more people, especially energetic achievers like you.)
Is this a stable and mature company? (A dependable, solid contributor
like you will be able to increase profitability whilst maintaining quality
and improving customer satisfaction.) Is the organisation in turmoil
or in turnaround mode? (Your dynamic, thinking-outside-the-box
process-improvement experience will pay dividends.)

Your condition

Your skills

Do you offer a unique combination of skills and experience that makes
you more valuable? Having a track record of success in dealing with
the kinds of issues this company currently faces makes you a very
desirable candidate and, of course, significantly increases your value.
Your mission is to tout those skills and experiences so that they don't
forget what a catch you are!

Your competition

Are they evaluating lots of other candidates? Are you on the short
list? Have they let it slip that they haven't even come close to finding

someone similar to you? Even if they've admitted there's no one else that can do what you do, it's still not a dead cert. Sell yourself until the bitter end.

Career path

Before you commit yourself to a potential contract that locks you in with a company for a specific time (which is often the case as a condition of sign-on bonuses), make sure you are satisfied that this company can provide you with an acceptable career path. If you are agreeing to a two-year contract to get a £3,500 bonus and it's clear that in the next two years there will be little or no room for advancement and that your best hope for a pay rise is, at best, an annual cost of living adjustment, think twice before doing it. Is a little bit of money now worth your potential freedom of options in six months or a year?

Win-Win

The best scenario for a lasting and happy relationship between you and your new employer is to end up with a situation that is win-win for both of you. Don't take your new employer to the cleaners during the salary and sign-on negotiations. If the employer is as happy with the final outcome as you are, they will treat you fairly and want to keep you around.

> 'Get what you're worth, but don't get greedy!'

If they feel that they've been cheated, it's very likely there will be some feelings of animosity floating around out there somewhere. That is never a recipe for a long and satisfying relationship. Get what you're worth, but don't get greedy!

9. Your Ongoing Job Search

(aka Your Second Career)

Congratulations! You found a job, you've negotiated a great salary, you like the benefits and the hours – everything's done! Or is it? Once the shine has worn off, that new job might not be what you thought it was. It's not uncommon for the honeymoon period to end as soon as you get comfortable at your new desk. The pressure is off as far as finding a job is concerned, and you might very well end up loving everything about this new role. But until you're sure you love it more than anything else in your life, don't end your job search! Keep your 'foot in the door'. Maintain contact with any potential leads that didn't come to fruition during your initial search. Don't lose contact with other companies that were trying to woo you. Keep your options open.

One of the mainstays of my business is repeat business! Sometimes a client will come back to do another job search only a couple of months after accepting what he thought was a great offer. The offer was great, but the job wasn't!

It's usually a case of the employer not living up to the expectations presented during the courtship period. Even if you've got everything in writing, there's no guarantee that they can deliver on their promise. (I've also had lots of clients who had the urge to move to a new location but, after being there for a short time, realised they hated the place! Always be sure you genuinely like a city before you commit to moving there.)

Sometimes the problem is more subtle: the client just isn't as excited about the job as he thought he'd be. That doesn't mean he should give up the job and look for something else. Quite the opposite. You are now employed, and that makes you a much better candidate than when you were unemployed. Now is a perfect time to look for something better. You aren't desperate, you know what your minimum requirements are to be happier (something greater than what you have now), and you have the luxury of time being on your side. Often the interviewing and deliberation and courting phases for the good jobs take longer than for the not-so-good jobs that a company is desperate to fill!

The other scenario for my repeat business, and a motivation for you to keep looking, is this: jobs don't last forever any more. The health and longevity of a company is, more often than not, completely out of your hands. A company's loyalty to its employees just isn't what it used to be, and the company money men love to lay people off by the thousands – that way it's nothing personal, just an aspect of business. (But why do they never lay off the money men?)

Keeping The Job Search Simmering

If companies approached you during your initial job search campaign, but nothing materialised into a job offer, these are still hot prospects! Quite often a company will approach a candidate because the candidate looks promising, even if they don't have a position available at that time. It's also quite common for a newly formed job (especially one that was being created specifically with you, or someone similar to you, in mind) to take several weeks, even months, to get approval, funding, and so on.

Most of the time, you just didn't have the luxury of waiting for these new positions to come to fruition. The good news is that you now have the time! Follow up on these opportunities, make sure they know you're still interested, and keep them excited and motivated so they'll wade through all the red tape and get the position ready.

Keep Alternative Offers On The Table

Play their game (aka 'the boss is away on holiday' game) against them. You might have had one or two, or maybe more, alternative offers that you were playing, one against the other, and, if you've played your cards right, those opportunities are still out there. Don't feel guilty about keeping them hanging on; it's very likely that they think they were/are still using the same routine on you.

That's OK at this point, because it works to your advantage. Keep the ball in motion; make follow up phone calls on a regular basis so they don't forget about you. Make enquiries about whether they have anything else that would be a fit for you. (This is a great way of networking.)

> 'Never burn your bridges, regardless of the situation; there are no advantages and lots of perils.'

If you were in the middle of negotiations with a company but decided to accept an offer from someone else and are now regretting your decision, call the other company back. It's very possible that they haven't filled the vacancy yet. Don't feel that you're the villain of the piece because you walked away from the negotiations; just tell yourself you were playing a tough game. If they're really interested in you, they'll take you back. The key to success in your job search, and every other aspect of your life, is to treat the people you're dealing with courteously, professionally and with respect. If you gave them a reasonable explanation for walking away from the last round of negotiations, they'll have no reason not to want to talk to you again.

The Ongoing Job Search: Your Second Career

Even if you completely love your new job, don't fully switch off from your job search. Unfortunately, in this day and age, the chances of you working for that company up until it's time to get the gold watch and ride off into the sunset are virtually nil. In fact, the chances of making it to your five-year anniversary aren't that great.

Keep your job search simmering in the background so you have an escape plan in place. Every few months, update your CV. It's a great practice to get into because it helps you keep focused on your strengths and successes, plus you can use it in presenting your case for a pay rise. Once you have that CV updated, get it back into circulation. As with a full-blown job search, a spectacular CV will do you absolutely no good if it isn't being seen.

Finally, A Use For The Job Websites!

Congratulations! You are now one of the millions of passive job-seekers cluttering the job boards. Throw your CV out there with everyone else. Think of it as one of those holiday fishing trips. You know, the ones where about 200 clueless tourists stand around the edges of a 60-foot boat, elbow-to-elbow with their fellow 'anglers'? Everyone has a rented fishing rod, baited with a hunk of frozen fish meat, and drops their line straight down next to their neighbour's hook. I actually caught a fish once! It could happen; the law of numbers says so. Of course I'm referring to the law of really big numbers. In other words, even though it's highly unlikely that you will find your dream job drifting in a sea of CVs, if you cast enough of them out onto the waters, someone, somewhere, might see you and take the bait!

Job boards are free, they're easy to use, and you can use the tools that they provide to make the process almost maintenance-free, so by all means, do it! Just don't expect spectacular results fast.

Don't Let Recruitment Consultants Trick You Into Joining Their Database

As soon as you put your CV on a job board, you will undoubtedly be approached by recruitment consultants. (Job boards are the primary hunting grounds of recruiters, marketing scammers, and 100% commission employers.) If a recruiter approaches you and says that he has an opportunity for you, make him give you the specifics before you agree to let him represent you. It's all too likely he doesn't have a single thing for you; he just wants to add you to his list of candidates. That means that if you stumble across an opportunity while surfing the job boards, and he was lucky enough to have sent your CV to them first, he can collect his commission when you get the job. Quite often, a recruiter will have an agreement with a company that states that, if the company chooses to recruit an individual that was represented by the recruiter at any time, they have to pay him a commission, even if they didn't recruit the candidate for the position that the recruiter originally presented the candidate for! Those agreements can last anywhere from 30 days to a year or more.

Keep A List Of Everyone You Had Contact With In Your Last Job Search

This is your REAL network. Your friends, colleagues, and family are probably barely on speaking terms with you right now if you tried to use them during your last job search, but that's OK because they were a poor network to begin with. Your real network is the list of companies (and the people you encountered within them) that you created in your job search campaign.

That is a goldmine of networking opportunities! Those are all people you can call on again to search for hidden treasure. It is a circle of people much bigger than you've ever had previously, and they aren't your friends and relatives, uncomfortable with being stuck in the middle of your depressing search for a job. Instead they're professional acquaintances you've only interacted with professionally. So they aren't under pressure if they give you a lead. (Imagine what goes through the mind of friends or family members when they recommend you to their manager. 'Is he going to mess up the interview and make me look bad?' Or worse, 'What if I recommend him to my boss, he takes the job and then falls apart. How am I going to look?') Instead, when they make a recommendation to a boss or business acquaintance, they can honestly say that they have spoken to you and reviewed your CV and that, though they were impressed, they just didn't have an appropriate vacancy, but they felt that you would make a great addition to X team or to so-and-so's department. The pressure is off, so they're more likely to help.

Know Your Rights: Non-Competes Can't Compete!

A non-compete or no competition agreement is generally used when an employee is an expert in a technical area or has a high degree of product-specific knowledge, and if they were to go to the competition, they could potentially wreak havoc on their previous employer. It is, in essence, an insurance policy with the beneficiary being the employer.

All too often, that non compete can be potentially harmful or even devastating to your career. (If the non-compete says you can't work in your industry for two or three years, how would that affect your overall career? I can't think of any way it would help your career.)

Review any non-compete contracts BEFORE you sign them. Ideally, you should ask a lawyer to look at it. The good news is that most non-competes don't hold up well in court, especially if they're too restrictive. The courts usually look at the non-compete from the viewpoint of fairness:

1   Does the employer need to protect a legitimate business interest? (In most companies, everybody gets a non-compete, regardless of the need or legitimacy of the contract.)

2   Would this contract place undue hardship on the employee? (If you are an engineer, for example, and the non-compete says you can't work as an engineer for two years after leaving them, you would essentially be unemployed for that time. Most courts would not enforce that. Of course, they might ask you why you would agree to that!)

3   Could taking a job in the same field or industry cause injury to the public?

4   What are the geographic restrictions? If the agreement covers the entire country, the courts are much less likely to enforce the contract. Typically, when a judge reviews the case, he is looking at this both from the viewpoint of the company trying to protect their business, and from the individual trying to support his or her family.

5   Are the competitors named or clearly defined? If not, it would be very difficult to prevent you from working for a competing company, because there is no way to prove that it really is a competitor. Is a supplier or support business really a competitor? These are some of the key points you should consider, both before signing a non-compete agreement and before looking for a new job.

DISCLAIMER: I am not a legal expert. Although I may have a
smooth tongue and a natural propensity for nonsensical banter,
I am not a trained, legal professional! Always consult your doctor,
don't try these stunts at home, no animals were harmed in the writing
of this book.

10. Your Marketing Approach

You Don't Have One!

Until now, you've been walking around in the dark. Very few, if any, job-seekers have a legitimate, well-thought-out marketing plan in place before they start looking for work. A job search is identical to a full-on sales campaign. Every basic principle of sales and marketing applies to your reemployment marketing campaign. The three basic ingredients of the successful job search marketing plan are:

1 *Product* In this case, YOU and your CV/covering letter. Think of yourself as the latest breakfast cereal. You are the delicious little bits of sugar-coated, sugar-filled, sugar flakes; and your CV and covering letter are the eye-catching box on the shelf, with the healthy, slim person eating what looks like a nutritious breakfast of pure sugar!

2 *Market* The companies that would be a great fit for your skills and experience, and the right person within those companies (the recruiting decision-makers).

3 *Spotlight* Getting your product into the spotlight by exposing it to enough people, in the right positions, to generate enough activity within an acceptable time frame to get your next job!

Those are the basic tenets of a good marketing campaign. If your plan includes bombarding recruiters with your CV via email, posting your CV on every free job site you can find, and responding to every ad in the paper whilst nagging your friends and family about leads, you are no doubt reading this book because your job search is poor! Of course, the best marketing plan can't guarantee great sales. For every successful marketing campaign, there is an equally important sales plan. Once you've generated activity from your marketing efforts, it is critical you have the proper sales tools available to ensure that you close the deal.

A solid sales plan includes:

- *Interviews* Make sure you have a plan for both phone and face-to-face interviews. This is the actual sales process. The CV opened the door; the interviews are what actually sell you. Prepare an outline for both the initial screening call interview and the multiple interviews with ascending levels of management in the companies you are approaching.

- *Follow-up* Not every sale is struck on the first try; every successful salesman knows that the bulk of his business comes from tenacity and solid follow-up work. Thank-you letters, phone calls, and a persistent approach to every lead is what gets you the results you want. Don't be lazy and withdrawn now; save that for when you get the job and they're stuck with you.

- *Negotiations* Once they say yes, don't roll over and accept something that is less than the best. A good sale becomes a great sale once you throw in all the extras and insurance to cover the time between when the insurance should start and when it actually does start. The devil is in the detail, especially when it comes to negotiating the perks that will make you truly love your new job.

'A great sales plan will ensure that the efforts of your marketing plan pay the dividends you expect.'

Your Marketing Materials

Bad CVs: from poor writing to horrible gimmicks

The key part of your job search is your CV, both from a marketing perspective, as this is the primary tool you'll be using to generate activity, and from the view point of sales, as this will be the salesman who will keep on selling you after you've done a brilliant job in the interview and have left the building. It has a huge weight on its shoulders, unimaginable responsibility, and the capacity to send your career skyrocketing – and yet, is usually the worst thing going in your search! Generally, it's not your fault. I place the blame squarely on 'they'. They told you to put your personal statement at the top, they said that you can't have more than one page, they said just to list all of your best achievements and not to tell them when or where or how they occurred. They made a lot of suggestions, and none of them were based on practical experience or insider knowledge.

Most of the drivel being shovelled out to job-seekers with regard to CVs is just recycled rubbish that was bad when it was invented and is just as dodgy 20 years later. They don't know what they're talking about! Every bit of information I put into CVs for my clients is put there for a reason. It was learned from years of working with both the job-seekers and the recruitment decision-makers throughout the life cycle of a job search. None of it was invented in a vacuum; when I make a suggestion to clients, I also give them an explanation. I explain why they were told to do certain things in their CV that are actually useless, unnecessary, and, sometimes, harmful. My goal is to give you the knowledge to understand why you've done the things you've done in your CV, and why you shouldn't be doing them!

Know your audience: the cynical reader

The first thing to understand about the reader of your CV – and I am referring to the recruitment decision-maker at the right level for the job you're going for, NOT your friends, family, colleagues, or recruiters (more about that in a minute) – is that he is a very cynical person. I say that because we are all cynical when you get right down to it. If we are reading something about someone and there is a piece of information missing, we naturally assume the worst. It's human nature. Deny it as much as you want, but I am cynical enough to know that you're lying. The reader is a busy person. His first plan with your CV will be to quickly scan through it looking for the 'aha'. By that I mean that he will skim through your CV until he can say, 'Aha, I knew there was a reason why I didn't want to waste any more of my valuable time on this person!' If you leave out the answer to any of his questions, he will have the perfect opportunity to answer them for you, and it will be a bad answer.

I said that your CV is being written for a very specific audience: the recruitment decision-maker – NOT your friends and family or your colleagues, and definitely not recruitment consultants, because they are simply not the right audience for a good CV.

Your friends and family

You'll want to show your CV to family, and they will want to give you good feedback, because they love you and want to help you. They can't really do you much good (but they can certainly harm you, unintentionally) for two main reasons.

One: they don't have a clue about what should go into a CV to motivate a recruitment decision-maker to pick up the phone and invite you in to discuss a position that could, potentially, have a major impact on their business. It's not likely that your spouse is the CEO of a major company. And, even if he or she was, your spouse knows you too well.

Two: when you know an individual, as I'm sure your friends and family do, you subconsciously 'fill in the blanks' when you read about that person. We all do it.

Your colleagues

Yes, they work in the same field as you, they know what a great person you are and they've recruited people before. But have they ever recruited someone at your level? Are they impressed with the CV because of what they see, or because they know you and see what isn't really there? Is your techie workmate excited about your CV because it talks about the 'Alphabet Soup' jargon that you and he chat about? Your future employer isn't likely to be nearly as impressed with technical mumbo-jumbo, especially if he isn't a computer geek. He might be intimidated by it or just put off. He would rather know how you used a can of Alphabet Soup to improve the productivity and profitability of the company.

Recruitment consultants

This CV isn't for recruitment consultants. Recruiters have a totally different game plan for your CV. To the recruiter, your CV is another asset for their database, so he wants it in a very specific format so that he can easily shove it into the right section. When the time comes that he needs to throw a handful of CVs at a job that you'd fit, he wants to be able to quickly scan your CV and find the superficial specs that would justify his having thrown you at the position. (And of course, he wants to keep your CV as short as possible. That way it reduces the pressure on his storage space, the amount of paper he wastes and gives him less information to read.) If a recruiter tells you your CV is bad and starts making all kinds of 'recommendations' to improve it, ignore him.

If you are working with a recruiter who has a genuine opportunity for you, and he asks that you change your CV to help him promote you better to potential employers, feel free to make the changes. He is presumably trying to help you, so you should try to help him. But don't think that just because he suggested a change that you have a bad document; you just didn't have a document that fitted the template that recruiters use to easily move thousands of CVs a month. If your goal is to become one of the anonymous masses flowing through the stream of recruiters, then you'll definitely want to knock your CV down to one page, use the top half of that single page for a generic summary section, and fill in the bottom third with buzzwords.

Your CV: All The Usual Suspects

Achievement-based. Keyword tables. Hiding your age. Forcing the reader to believe you graduated and got your first job as Director at IBM. And last but not least, the one-size-fits-all summary section!

There are several styles of CVs floating around out there that came about in the late 1980s, a time when professionals suddenly found themselves out on the streets through no fault of their own or were moving from job to job because the corporate world was in turmoil. Hostile takeovers, the flourishing love of redundancies, downsizing, reductions in force, blah blah blah – the gimmicky catchphrases abounded, and lots of good people were left to look for work.

They had lots of perceived issues to overcome, including their age and the fact that their career had already peaked and was now on the downhill slide. They were encountering the first generation of automated HR, and recruiters were the great-white hunters, making a killing, charging bundles and inventing the rules as they went along. Several phenomena occurred because of these factors.

'Company Director as a first job' CVs

Older workers, who for their entire lives had operated under the belief that it was not only possible but certain that they would work for their company until retirement, were suddenly laid off. They were now in the race for a new job with a gaggle of younger recruits. The fear of age discrimination led to the birth of the 'Company Director as a first job' CVs. The thinking was: tell the reader what you've done for the last 10 years or so, WOW them with your actions and abilities, and quietly leave out the 15 years of experience that came before that. Hopefully, the reader will be so impressed with what he sees, he'll completely overlook the fact that your first job was one that is usually reserved for a seasoned veteran. Maybe it worked in the beginning, but your manager soon caught on! It quickly became obvious what older job-hunters were doing, so now, when a recruitment decision-maker sees a CV using this trick, he automatically assumes you've lopped off at least 10 years from your age, and he is left to believe that you think that you are too old for the job. Age discrimination is illegal, but it is still practised. Often, the people who suffer from it are not the ones who realise that they are still vital and can make extremely valuable contributions to a company and go forward with a positive attitude. The ones who suffer the greatest discrimination are often those people who don't realise their value and inadvertently send a signal to the reader that age is a factor. Keep this in mind as you put your CV together and concentrate on highlighting your skills and knowledge to show recruiter how much valuable experience you can bring to the role.

Achievement-based CVs (aka 'Look out, my career is almost over')

The concept of the achievement-based CV is: list all your greatest accomplishments, most impressive results and highest praises, and then, at the bottom of the CV, tick off the various companies you've worked for and make the reader guess where you were successful. Of course, the reader has no idea if these are achievements that you've generated in the last five years, or 15 years ago. It's a sorry ploy, and it's the first thing he'll want to clarify, if he's actually motivated to talk to you at all. This means that you will be trapped in an interview, avoiding the facts as much as you can, realising that you have egg on your face because you somehow thought you could get away with it. Don't worry. This will rarely happen to you, as most employers are extremely familiar with this style of CV. It's quite frequently paired off with the 'Company Director as first job' CV. They will see it for what it really is: a giant billboard advertising your downhill slide. 'But wait', you say, 'my career isn't going down the pan!' Bad luck – that's what you've told the reader.

Maybe your career is on the downhill slide. You still have to tell the reader what you've done most recently; play up the success and quickly move on to the next position. Hopefully, you aren't that far past your glory days. If you are, it may be time to re-evaluate your goals.

Buzzword CVs

With the birth of the technological revolution, CVs became easier for the average man or woman in the street to create, and more and more of them began to flood the job market. Companies were also able to capitalise on the emerging technologies and found ways to cope with the growing number of CVs arriving at their HR departments. Scanners were one of the primary tools first used. An HR drone could run all the CVs through the scanner and rely on software to pick up keywords that would then allow them to place the CV in the right pile for later shuffling.

The first scanners and the software for them were really poor, so the trend began for CV writers to add keyword tables, or what they eventually morphed into: buzzword buckets. Take all the trendy 'in-words' and put them in smart-looking bulleted tables. What do they mean? How do they relate to you? Why should anyone care about those words!? Who knows!? Presumably, they catch the software's attention and tell the reader you're completely up to date with all the important buzzwords in your industry, making you the best candidate for the job.

One-page to two-page CVs (aka 'Plus 20 years' additional experience')

To this day, this is the one piece of advice that I hear most often bandied about, fought over, and viciously defended. However, almost no-body I talk to can give me the real reason there are so many one- or two page CVs floating around out there. The most popular theory I hear is that the reader is very busy and you only get 15 seconds, or 10 seconds, or five seconds, or even no seconds at all to tell them everything they need to know!

Are you really that naive? Do you genuinely believe that a recruitment manager is only going to give five seconds, or even 60 seconds of thought and consideration to recruiting you? Yes, she's a busy woman and, yes, she does want to know quickly why you're bothering her, but, if she's even mildly interested, she also wants to know who you really are and what value you could bring the company. That's why the covering letter is there: to quickly and succinctly introduce you and explain why you should be considered.

The truth of the origin of the one- or two-page CV is that recruiters use CVs for their database figures and bulky, longwinded CVs are more difficult to file away and take up more space. Also, when 'professional CV writers' came onto the scene, it made sense to keep the CV as short as possible. If they can convince their customer that a one-page CV – which he can churn out in 15 minutes

– is worth hundreds of pounds because he has his finger on the pulse of the industry, their profit margins go through the roof. At no point in the equation do the merits of the candidate and his CV come into consideration!

One-size-fits-all summary section

My personal favourite in the world of CVs is the one with the first third of the page consumed with a one-size-fits-all summary section! I can't think of anything more useless on your CV. Call it what you like (executive summary, overview, synopsis, whatever). It should really be called: Hollow Claims Made by Every Single Person on the Planet! I have read that summary section about 50 thousand times and not once was it original, impressive, informative, entertaining, engaging, appealing, winning, charming or in any way whatsoever helpful in letting me know who you were! It's a waste of space. If you can't effectively demonstrate all those claims you're making in your CV by telling the reader what you've done in your career, you are obviously lying about them! Show, don't tell. Don't be presumptuous enough to *tell* the reader what to think of you; be clever enough to *show* the reader what to think of you. Because the reader will be thinking that if you can't do it on paper, you probably won't be able do it on the job either.

Gaps: Were You In Prison Or In Rehab?

Remember: your reader is an extremely cynical one, so don't leave him any opportunities to think the worst of you. Gaps are the kiss of death in your CV. The sad part is that in most instances they are there not because the job-seeker was unemployed, but because they were careless in the creation of their documents and totally overlooked the discrepancy in dates. Your laziness will bite back every time. If you have genuine gaps in your CV, make every effort to explain them. If you took a year off to have a child, in your 'Reason for Leaving' section of the job prior to having your baby, explain that you left to take care of your child during the critical first year. If you spent a year and a half between jobs backpacking across Asia, in your next position, explain that you took the job after a short sabbatical to travel abroad. (Don't be tempted to share your adventures; just acknowledge the gap, give a reasonable explanation, and move on.)

Bullet Points: Do You Only Speak In Clipped Sentences At The Top Of Your Voice?

BULLET POINTS IN YOUR CV IS THE SAME AS EMAILING YOUR FRIENDS IN CAPITAL LETTERS. YOU ARE SHOUTING AT THE TOP OF YOUR VOICE, METAPHORCALLY SPEAKING, AND YOU ARE USING BROKEN SENTENCES THAT DON'T TELL A STORY. HOW MUCH MORE OF THIS COULD YOU STAND? I would throw this book down immediately if it looked like this! Bullet points are for facts and figures; bullets are NOT for communicating complex ideas and thoughts. It's similar to reading an instruction manual for complex engineering software: it's boring, it's impossible to comprehend and nobody reads it! It's just the same for your boring, bulleted CV.

And while we're on the subject of bullets: don't use arty bullet points – you know, the little stars or horseshoes or moons. They're completely unprofessional, many computers don't have the font installed (so yours will be replaced with goodness knows what), and it just looks silly. This is a CV, not a flyer inviting your friends to a party!

Why You Should Never Put Your Picture On Your CV

Discrimination on the basis of age, sex, nationality, and race is illegal. Companies are scared to death of being accused of it. So, when you put a photo of yourself on your CV, the only thing you're succeeding in doing – apart from giving the HR drone a perfect target for his or her doodles – is making it extremely difficult for the employer to consider you. They know that if they call you and then don't recruit you, you could accuse them of discrimination based on whatever they saw in your picture. It's so much safer and easier for them to just throw that ticking time bomb away and pretend that it never happened, than to tempt fate by touching it! Unless you are applying for the lead role in a soap opera, a picture of yourself is the last thing you should ever include.

Are You Spamming Your Next Employer? Or: How The Digital Revolution Is Contributing To Your Unemployment

Is it the digital revolution or just another gimmick to get your 30 quid? There are probably dozens of companies on the net selling this service and I won't say they're a scam, because they do generally provide the service that they advertise, which is to broadcast your CV to hundreds or even thousands of recruiters who may work in your industry. From that perspective, they're totally legitimate. However, if you engage in that service under the impression that you will be generating any level of results, you're very likely to be disappointed. And if you are hanging on to your chances of finding your next job based on the sole efforts of a recruiter that might receive your CV from that email blast, you need a reality check.

In the past, I have experimented by placing myself on the lists for those spammers – I mean, email blaster services – and let me warn you: You are not the only one being blasted! I received two hundred CVs on a light day to a record day of 4,798! Needless to say, I didn't have a clue what to do with all those CVs, so I promptly deleted them. Most recruiters sign up for the email broadcasters, as well as specialist industry sources, so they get thousands of electronic CVs and hundreds of paper CVs every week. Why do they do this? Because it's free, it gives them an endless supply of free sales leads (remember that their entire database is made up of people like you), and, the more candidates that they can draw in, the greater their likelihood of placing one of them.

Emailing

If you do manage to get past HR, are you spamming your next manager? It would be difficult to find an accurate list of email addresses for recruiting decision-makers out there. Why? Because they don't want you emailing them! Isn't a hundred emails for Viagra enough for a day? Do you honestly think they also want to have to go through their in-box looking for unsolicited (read: spam) CV submissions? It's much easier to hit the delete button than to work out who you are and why you're approaching them. Even if they do take the time to look at the email, your submission will seem very lazy and they'll feel that you're not really a serious job-seeker. They know how easy and free emails are, so why should they be impressed that you emailed them your CV? If you emailed it to them, then you obviously also emailed it to everyone else on the planet. DELETE. Email is an OK, but not great, form of communication, once you've established a dialogue with a potential employer, but for a first impression it's very poor. If you're still tempted to use it, it must be because you're lazy and cheap – and that's what your potential employer will think.

Faxing

It all goes to HR, so why did you bother? Faxing your CV to a list of companies is as lazy and cheap as emailing, except this time you managed to get past the recruitment decision-maker and get your CV straight onto the desk of the HR drone. Good job!

11. Your Career Choices

Why Are You Looking For Work?

Self-analysis

Before you can find a new job that will make you happy, it's important that you fully understand what makes you unhappy. Taking away all, or at least as many as possible, of the things that make the job horrible will leave you with a job that will make you happy. Or will it? Sometimes, the real reason you hate your job isn't what it appears to be. You may think you hate your current job because your manager is an idiot and asks you to do more than you should have to. Although it is certainly possible that your boss is an uncaring, slave-driving fool, there's a good chance that the real reason you don't like your boss is because he or she makes you do work that you just don't like. That means that the boss isn't the villain of the piece; the work is. It might just be time to re-analyse what your career interests are. If you aren't at least alright with getting up in the morning to do your job, then there's something wrong. Do you really like what you do? Does it excite you? Does it make you glad you did it? Do you sometimes want to pinch yourself because this is what you've always dreamed of doing?

Your Industry, Your Role: Are You 'Stuck In A Rut'?

If the answer is no, then ask yourself: 'Am I dissatisfied with my job because of who I work with, or because of what I do?' Truthfully ask yourself: 'If the boss were the greatest person in the world, would I be happy doing the work?' If you can't honestly tell yourself that it's the work you love, then it's time to re-evaluate your current career track. Don't get me wrong. I'm not advocating that you should drop your job making a hundred grand a year to try out for Manchester United. I'm just saying that if selling annuities to yuppies is completely boring you, consider selling pharmaceuticals. Maybe intangibles aren't your thing. Keep selling; but sell something that excites you. It's the same for being a secretary. Maybe it's not the fact that your boss is an idiot;

maybe it's just that you can't stand legal work. Find a doctor's office to work in. Change the pace, but not necessarily the track.

Did You Get Downsized?

Are you in a shrinking industry? If you got laid off, downsized, reduction-in-workforce-ed (pick your favourite euphemism for 'deemed unprofitable'), it's time to re-evaluate your industry. Are you sticking with an industry that's sinking? Are you still manufacturing widgets, even though China and Pakistan are now the worldwide leaders in widget production? Are you still listening to tapes in your car and watching videos? Change hurts some of us. An excellent book called *Who Moved My Cheese?* by Spencer Johnson does a great job of explaining this type of person. Basically, the premise of the book is that there are three types of people: Those who accept change when it comes and move along with it; those who accept change only with great reluctance and after suffering minor hunger pangs; and those who can't stand the thought of change and will sit in their
little corner of the rat maze, waiting for their cheese to be put back where it's always been. Those are the ones who will wither away to nothing and starve to death, rather than accepting the fact that their hunk of cheese has been moved and it isn't coming back.
Read the book; it will definitely help you get a handle on who you are. If you are still trying to get rich with stocks and shares in your dotcom business, there's an email in your inbox with the subject line 'Get over it!'

Are You Unhappy With Your Challenges?

Sometimes, getting a new job isn't the answer. Rather than making a complete leap, the secret to your happiness might be as simple as going to your manager and telling him that you just don't think there are enough challenges in your job. Ask for more responsibility. Believe it or not, your manager will probably be delighted to give you more! This also speaks volumes about the kind of high quality employee you are. When you go out and find more work to do, accept more challenge and responsibility than your colleagues, contribute at a higher level than expected, who do you think they will consider first when promotion opportunities come along? It definitely won't be Rob, the bloke two desks down from you who gets to work five minutes late, takes an extra 10 minutes for lunch, and then leaves five minutes early at the end of the day.

Not Getting Paid Enough?

Have you asked your current employer for a pay rise yet? If you said no and instead you're looking for another job to get more money, I must ask, 'What's wrong with you?' Step one in getting more money: ask for it!

If you've already asked for more money and they said no, why did they say no? Is it because they can't afford to or are they too stingy? Or is it because the work that you do doesn't merit more pay? If you have reached the 'glass ceiling' for your current position, it may be time to make a move, but I always recommend trying to get to the next level first.

Try making a change within the company you're at now before you look for a new job somewhere else. You've got seniority, you know the rules and the politics, and you've got a foot in the door!

Are You Afraid To Take The Next Step Up The Ladder? (Or Is Something Holding You Back?)

Making the move can be scary. Asking your boss to promote you can be an intimidating concept. You might think it's easier just to go to another company and get a job at the next level. You might be right. It is certainly a proven method for career advancement. But again, moving up the career ladder is something you could quite possibly do just as easily with your current employer. You definitely won't know if it's possible or not until you try.

Have A Workable Plan In Place Before You Walk Into The Manager's Office.

Don't just walk in and demand that you be promoted or you're out of this dump! Sit down with a notepad and make a list of the qualities and skills you have that you think justify your promotion. List examples of the additional tasks and responsibilities that you have taken on that demonstrate that you are up to the challenge of a higher position. If you can't list any skills or any examples of the things you've done to demonstrate your worthiness, why on earth should you get a promotion?

> 'Understanding the root of your problem will guide you to the solution.'

Finding a job that will fulfil you means understanding what makes you happy – and what makes you unhappy. Thinking the grass is greener on the other side is a recipe for a constant search for happiness. It's very possible you'll never to find the right thing. You'll end up hopping from job to job, unsatisfied time and again, never realising that you could have been happy any number of times, if only you knew what you wanted.

12. The Scary Truth About the 'Holy Trinity'!

After helping people look for work for 10 years and talking to more than 50,000 job-seekers, I've learned that they all use the same three poor methods. And every one of them tells me that they don't work – but they keep using them because they just don't know any better. I call those methods for looking for work the 'Holy Trinity' because every job-seeker uses these techniques as if they were the divine answer to all of their problems! Job-seekers are convinced that if they devote enough time and work diligently using these sanctified methods of job-seeking, it will ultimately bring them the salvation they seek (a new job).

When everyone around you is using the same route to find their next job, and everyone around you is having trouble, don't you think it might be the wrong route? Just because they are the traditional methods for looking for work doesn't mean they are the only methods, or even the best. They're just the ones that everyone falls into because they are cheap, easy, and don't require a great amount of investment of time, money or thought.

The 'Holy Trinity' consists of job websites, networking and recruitment consultants. I bet you've been using them in your job search, and I bet that at this point you have finally given up on them. (Or you wouldn't be reading this book – you'd be too busy with all the great job opportunities, wouldn't you?) During the initial client interview at my company, one of the first questions asked is about what the client is currently doing to generate activity in his job search and, invariably, every single person we talk to says exactly the same thing. It's rare that they even change the order or the words: 'Oh, I've been on Monster and Careerbuilder and I've been doing a lot of networking for opportunities, and I'm working with a couple of recruitment consultants who say they have something for me, maybe soon . . .'

Depending on how far into the job search they are, they say this enthusiastically because they are so proud they are covering all the bases so effectively or, if they have been at it for a month or two, they start saying it with that ironic, 'I'm-starting-to-regret-saying-this' tone of voice. Most of the clients I talk to who have been using this approach for more than a few weeks are already becoming disillusioned.

When we follow up with the question of how the client would rate their job search success so far, they will usually respond with a smattering of false bravado, saying that it's going pretty well and there's been a lot of activity. But when you ask for clarification (do they mean that they have been getting a lot of interviews and job offers?), they all say no, just lots of emails that their CV has been received and is under review, or they're getting lots of calls from sales people and commission-only financial and insurance sales. (They all seem confused about why an insurance or financial services company would approach them when they have no background in those industries. Well, it's because those industries survive on the sale of their products to your friends and family! The turnover rate in those companies is astronomical. If you sell a policy to two of your family members before giving up and quitting, they win.) Even for the slowest job-seeker, it doesn't take more than six or eight weeks to realise that the Holy Trinity of job searching is a more arduous path than the search for the Holy Grail.

Each one of those methods has its merits. Don't get me wrong. I'm not recommending that you avoid them completely. I'm just saying that if you are relying on them as your main way to find work, you may well be at the search much longer than you expected. Let me explain.

Job Websites: Why You And 3 Million Other Disgruntled Employees Aren't Getting Recruited

In any given month, millions of people looking for work land on job websites like Careerbuilder and Monster hoping to be seen and heard in the race for a new job. Many of those people are what are called 'passive job-seekers'! This is a politically correct term for 'disgruntled;

annoyed-at-their-boss-on-Monday; not-really-looking-for-a job-BUT-would-consider-it-if-it-landed-in-their-lap-and-pays-twice-as-much-as-their-current-role job-board surfers'.

So why do the websites do what they do? Do you think they're providing this service out of charity? Er, no. Do you think that they make their money simply by providing a meeting place for job-seekers and employers? No again! Yes, they sell advertising space to hundreds of companies, but so do most major internet sites, and, OK, they sell job posting packages to legitimate companies looking to fill vacancies. But a huge percentage of their revenue is generated by selling access to their database of CVs to people who see you as a huge pool of SALES LEADS!

'Win a free trip to telemarketing hell!'

Recruitment consultants, employment agencies, salespeople, franchisers, self-employment scam artists, insurance agents, investment advisors, estate agents – the list goes on and on. Imagine you ran a company that sold a service that could be used by someone in a particular industry, who may soon be moving, who is currently unhappy with their financial situation, or desperate to become re-employed. What better place to find them than by going to a company that specialises in collecting all the personal information they can about these people, people who are fresh on the scene, motivated, and ready to be sold to? Job websites are one of the most innovative and exciting sales lead generators to come along since the invention of the 'Win a Free Trip to _____' competition!

I'm amazed how many times I've talked to people who ask me, 'How did you get my information?' or who say, 'I'm being very discreet in my job search, so I don't want you to call me at my office', and yet they post their CV on the internet! That's almost the same as posting a picture of yourself and a gorgeous stranger (NOT your partner) on the web, and then being shocked when your friends and colleagues find out about it. Put your CV on a job website and you might as well put an advertising billboard up with all your personal information on it. It's out there, and anybody who wants it can have it.

'You're a serious job-seeker, agonising over your reply
to a job posting; the other 5,000 people who respond to it
are just fed up with their boss today.'

I'm also amazed how many prospects tell me that they usually spend
an hour or more crafting a personalised covering letter and making
tweaks to their CV before they submit it to a posting on a job board.
They just don't seem to realise that, while they were agonising over
the perfect way to express why they are the perfect candidate for the
job (by trying to guess at what the decision-maker is looking for,
then highlighting it in their CV and covering letter), hundreds if
not thousands of other, passive website-surfers have already emailed
their CV!

The typical way of working for 'passive job-seekers' is to submit
their CV to basically anything that pops up in front of them that
sounds even remotely more interesting than the boring job they have
now. They already realise that they aren't likely to get a response and,
even if they do get one, they aren't going to go for an interview unless
they can double their salary.

And here you are, spending half a day trying to impress the robot
that's going to be scanning your CV along with the thousand others
cluttering its inbox. Submit your CV, but don't spend all day doing
it. Take the same approach as the passive types because you'll get the
same results as them. Make the job websites part of your daily routine
while aggressively looking for work, but don't let them take up more
than an hour of your day. There are far more effective uses for your
time: networking through your list of companies, following up on
leads, sending thank-you letters . . .

HR Forgot The Posting Was Even There

In the course of my job, I quite often talk to HR professionals looking
for work. (There is a sense of irony there, but they need help just as
much as the next person, especially because they are already aware of
how daunting a task it is to get through the HR black hole!) I've been
told by many of these professionals that another reason they know
submitting their CV on job websites is so futile is because a shockingly

large number of the postings on those sites aren't even legitimate –
and they were posted by genuine companies! Apparently, all too often,
the postings you see on job websites are there because:

- The company has a contract with the site and is committed to
  a certain amount of monthly advertising, regardless of their
  recruitment needs. (This is the case with traditional news print
  adverts, as well.) So the company runs a generic ad just to fill
  space, and to trawl the web just looking for anybody interesting
  who might surface.
- The company is bound by certain equal opportunities
  requirements and, in an effort to meet those needs, they list
  job postings to legitimise themselves as having fulfilled certain
  minimum requirements. So they post ads for fictitious openings,
  and then file away the results so that, if they are ever audited,
  they can show that they did make an effort.
- A job is posted, and the HR department is overwhelmed with
  responses and chucks a load of CVs at the recruitment manager,
  who either employs one of them or goes with an internal candidate,
  but never informs HR. After a while HR forgets all about the
  posting (which is typically listed for three-month periods) and
  it is just left floating around in cyberspace, forgotten by all,
  but still generating hundreds of emailed CVs a day, which are
  usually discarded automatically to avoid having to deal with equal
  opportunities requirements. Regardless of the scenario, none of
  them do you any good, and yet you might very well be spending a
  large amount of time trying to craft the perfect response to it. Just
  post your CV and move on.

The Startling Reality Of Scanners: HR Never See The CVs Sent To Posting

OK, let's imagine you've submitted your CV, and it's ended up in
the in-box of a genuine job posting, at a real company that really is
looking to recruit a new employee. Great! Now, what are the chances
of it being seen by a human? Well, if it's a small company, the chances
are quite good, as they won't have the budget or inclination to invest

in or use sophisticated scanning software designed to analyse CVs and cull specific data assigned a value as to the appropriateness-level of a prospective candidate. Eh? Most large companies use scanners and specialised software to sift through the thousands of CVs they receive on a daily basis. It's too big a task for humans to do.

About six or seven years ago, I had a client who worked for a major car manufacturer. His job, along with three other people, was to go through the paper CVs that the company received every day and put them into the appropriate filing cabinet. He usually went through about 800 to 1,000 CVs a day and that, unless there was a specific phrase or set of criteria that the candidate included on his CV, the rest were thrown into boxes labelled 'TBNT-Factory', 'TBNT-Design', and so on.

The client was working with me to find a new job because progress had just passed him by, making his job obsolete, thanks to new and improved software. Nowadays, even that tiny level of human decision-making in larger companies has, quite often, been eliminated from the process. The even sadder truth is that, even if you make it past the software, you're now in the hands of an HR drone who is, typically, totally in the dark about what would make a good candidate, beyond the criteria arbitrarily included on the job description.

The black hole of HR

I once had a client; I'll say her name was Barbara. She was a Director of Operations for a large company. She had been with the company for several years and was quite happy with the job, the responsibilities and the pay. It was the commuting that was getting her down. She was driving an hour and a half, one way, twice a day. When she started working for the company the commuting was OK, but then they moved their head office and it started to become a real problem. About a year before Barbara contacted me, she had a baby. Now the commute was impossible. She explained the situation to her manager. Relocating wasn't a viable option, as her husband had an even higher-paying job, she had a stepson in school and all of her family lived in the same area. The only solution was to look for a new job. Her employer understood. They were sad to see her go, but she graciously offered to stay on board until the company was able to take on her replacement, and she even agreed to train the replacement.

The first step in finding a replacement was for Barbara to put together a job specification for the new director. She spent several days putting together a list of the qualities and skills that would make a great replacement. She took her shopping list to the HR department and explained what she was looking for, giving them her candidate specification to work from. After that Barbara went back to work, content in the knowledge that she would soon be screening candidates to replace her.

Three weeks went by, and nothing happened. Barbara called HR and asked if they had run the advert. They said yes; they ran it in both of the local papers and on three of the largest national job websites. Barb was flabbergasted. No responses? 'Oh, yes. There have been responses,' the HR drone tells her. 'Just none that fit the requirements list you gave us.'

Barbara was dejected. It was going to be tough to find a replacement. She kept her chin up and went back to work, knowing that there would be some good people, but that it just might take a little longer than she thought for them to come along.

Two more weeks went by, and still no candidates landed on her desk. She was getting really frustrated now. Barbara called the drones in HR and asked, 'Are there any candidates yet?' 'No. We've looked at about 1,200 CVs, but nothing matches.' Twelve hundred! This got Barbara thinking. She pulled out her own CV and crossed out her name, put her sister's name and mobile phone number on it, and submitted it to the HR department through one of the job board postings. This was on a Wednesday. By Friday she hadn't seen 'her' CV yet. She called the person in HR and asked if they had a chance to review so and-so's CV yet. The HR genius looked up the name and informed her that yes, they did review so-and-so's CV – and she didn't qualify!

Networking: Do You Have Any Friends Left?

If you call all your friends on Monday and they can't help, and you call all your friends again on Wednesday and they can't help, and you call all your friends again on Friday, how many of them are still taking your calls? The concept that networking is the best way to find your next job is an incredibly flawed one. Yes, networking can lead to a great job, and it probably will unearth potential opportunities, but it really is only a method to be employed if you have lots and LOTS of time to spend on your job search. Networking is not going to find you a job quickly. Your circle of influence and number of friends and acquaintances is unlikely to be large enough to find you a job at exactly the time that you need one. Networking only works if you network properly, which means you make consistent contact with your web of friends, colleagues, customers, neighbours and so on all the time.

Networking is an ongoing lifestyle, not a method for an aggressive job search with a goal of producing multiple job offers within a limited time frame. And if, or when, you try to use your network to that end, you will quickly find yourself losing more and more friends and associates. They will suddenly become swamped at work, always on the other line when you call, short with you on the phone, or, worse yet, walk the other way when they see you at a family function or on the street. That certainly isn't good for your morale, and usually the only results you get from your network are those informal interviews arranged as a favour for a friend. Spending time with executives discussing the job market and why they aren't really looking for someone right now, even though you are an incredibly talented person with loads to offer some lucky company, might make you feel a little better about yourself for an afternoon, but it does nothing to put cash in your bank account.

How many of your friends could employ you?

When you use your network to look for work, you're really waiting for someone to get fired, move on, or die. Those are the main circumstances in which your friends and colleagues would be able to help you in your job search. It's not as if you spend time with the executives of companies in your town. Or do you? If your network doesn't generally include executives at the same level as the people who can actually recruit you for a job, you're talking to the wrong people. A person at the same level as you knows as little as you about the inner workings and big-picture business development issues facing the management staff. If your best friend came to you today and asked you to point him or her to the right area of your company to get a job, who would you send them to? Human resources? Your mate, John? The CEO? Exactly! You wouldn't have a good answer for him or her, and you'd feel bad that you couldn't help your best friend. Now, imagine how you'll feel when your friend calls you again next week and asks you if you tracked down those opportunities you knew about. Would some have magically appeared? Would you feel even worse that you couldn't help your best friend in his or her time of need? Would you want to answer the phone the next time you see his or her name come up on your mobile phone?

> 'Your circle of influence rarely has any
> more influence than you, and you can't find yourself
> a job, so how could they?'

There are more than 2 million companies in the UK. Do you know someone at all of those companies? They are all companies you could potentially have a job with, based on your skills, experience and circumstances. Do you know someone at all of them? Half of them? One percent of them? Could you even name 500 companies?

I once had a client who told me, after he got a job at an athletic sock manufacturing plant, that he was very glad he had listened to me about not eliminating companies just because he couldn't picture himself there, because he would never have believed he'd get a job manufacturing socks! More often than not, your new job is at a company that you never even heard of before you went to work for them (unless you've spent your entire career only working for major companies). It's very likely that most of your friends and family had never heard of your last company before you told them you were working there.

Relying on your circle of acquaintances to identify a great job opportunity might seem a little futile, once you take into account that you are missing practically every job opportunity in the universe by relying solely on your friends to find you a job!

When does your network help and who is your real network?

Networking certainly has its place in your job search, and it would be foolish not to put your feelers out there, letting all your friends, family, colleagues and business acquaintances know either that you're unemployed or dissatisfied with your job and are looking for something better. Networking can be an effective addition to your job search when you include it as one facet of a much larger and more thorough, overall marketing campaign. Do it; just don't bet everything on it.

Your network will pay the greatest dividends when you use it as a part of your ongoing job search, the one that you should be continuing even after you find your next great job. (If you've forgotten what I'm talking about, revisit Chapter 9.) This is particularly true when you start to include your new network – the one that you'll be generating during this job search. Your new, and more valuable, network will be the people you come into contact with during this job search: the people you meet while you're at interviews, the people who call you just suss you out, even the people who you had an interview with, but who didn't take you on. These are people at a higher level than your current circle of friends. They aren't emotionally involved with you and they are more likely to be aware of future opportunities because they obviously, thought about making use of your talents at one point or they wouldn't have got in touch with you.

This group is your true network. But, as with any endeavour that includes digging a hole deep into the ground and then using a pickaxe to pry little nuggets of value out of rock, it takes a lot of time and effort. Don't expect miracles overnight but, have faith that, over time, with lots of work and patience, you are likely to strike it rich with these efforts.

Recruiters: The Good, The Bad, And The Ugly Truth

Every day I talk to people who think there is a recruitment consultant out there 'working for them'. What a laugh. If you had any concept of how recruiters work, and what conditions they face these days, you'd realise that you are placing your faith in a dark art. If a recruiter can place one person a week, he's doing a GREAT job! The industry statistics suggest that recruiters are responsible for placing employees in a very small number of the jobs filled each year. Yet, every day job-seekers are under the false impression that there is a recruiter out there working hard to find them a job.

The Difference Between Retained And Contingent Recruiters

The first thing to understand is that not every recruiter is created equal. There are two main categories of recruiters: retained and contingent. Retained recruiters have been brought in by a company to find candidates for a particular position. The employer is paying that recruiter to make the effort to find the candidates, screen them, and then arrange for the initial interviews with company recruitment managers. This type of recruiter is paid in advance for finding the candidate. He's motivated to quickly find someone that the company will accept, so that he can move on to his next contract.

The second type of recruiter, and the kind you are much more likely to encounter, is a contingent recruiter. These are recruiters who act as independent agents. They don't have a contract with a single company. Instead, they form relationships with as many companies as they can that are willing to see candidates put forward by that recruiter, understanding that if they employ a candidate introduced by him, the company will have to pay a commission to that recruiter. That commission can vary widely, but it is often a percentage of your initial annual salary. And that percentage can be quite significant. Depending on the type of vacancy he's filling and the difficulty involved, contingent recruiters can charge upwards of 20, 30 or even 40% your first year's salary! The company usually signs an agreement that commits that recruiter to any candidate they identify for as little as 30 days, to as long as six months or even a year. That means that if a recruiter presents you to a company for a position and you don't get the job for whatever reason, if you approached the company again in a few weeks, or even months, based on something entirely unrelated to the first job and with no help from that recruiter, the company would still be obliged to pay that recruiter his commission! He would get paid, even if it was for a totally different job, one that you perhaps found through the newspaper or a mailing campaign. You are his property once you agree to be represented by him. So it's better for the recruiter to be paid in advance. Retained is better than contingent is what I'm getting at.

The Dirty Tricks They Play (From 'The Good, The Bad, and The Ugly' To 'Getting You Fired So They Can Fill Your Position'!)

I don't want you to think that recruiters are awful, and I'm not saying that they all do terrible things to earn money, but you should be aware that they sometimes use methods that are less than scrupulous and are, sometimes, downright dirty.

One of the reasons that so many people get excited when a recruiter starts to 'work for them' is because they suddenly find themselves going to interviews. This seems very encouraging and, of course, it certainly gives you the feeling that things are really starting to happen! Now for the reality of the situation: The reason you suddenly find yourself going to lots of interviews and then, later, finding yourself waiting by the phone, expecting calls for follow-ups that never seem to happen, is because you were being used in the old game of the Good, the Bad, and the Ugly.

Let me explain it to you this way: imagine you want to buy a house. You find an estate agent and tell her what you're looking for: A three-bedroom, two bathroom house in a good neighbourhood with a nice school for your kids. You have a budget of around £200,000.

Now, the estate agent already has the perfect house for you. It instantly popped into her head, but she knows that if she drives you over there now, you might not be impressed enough with it, and she'll have to find another house. So, instead, she plays a game called the Good, the Bad, and the Ugly. The estate agent knows that the best way to make you fall in love with her first choice is to start by realigning your expectations. This means you get to go for a drive and walk around a couple of other houses first. The first house she takes you to is gorgeous! It's a three bedroom/two bathroom, and it has a huge secluded garden, a swing, and a jacuzzi at the back. Less than half a mile down the street is a great school, and there are neighbourhood watch signs everywhere.

You love it! It's perfect! You'll take it! How much? £400,000. What?!? Er, what else do you have? The Bad.

Back into the car, off to the next house. She takes you across the city, and you notice that the streets start to get a little narrower, and the lawns aren't quite as green. At last you pull up to another house, only this one seems to be a little older, maybe by a couple of decades. As you get out of the car, the estate agent happily informs you that this house is a bargain; it's listed for only £70,000, and the vendor is motivated. Hmm. You try to make the best of it, taking shallow breaths so the stench of mould and cat urine don't make you retch. Er, we were really thinking of something a little closer to the main road. The Ugly.

You get back in the car and start rummaging through your pockets, trying to remember if you slipped a bottle of air freshener in there. Now you remember why you hate looking for houses. It's depressing. On the drive back across town, the estate agent pulls out her list of houses and pretends to look through it, muttering to herself that she swears there was another house, not more than a mile away from the first one, that just came on to the market and, if she remembers correctly, it was a three bedroom/two bathroom – ah, here it is! It's listed for £240,000, but she's sure you could make an offer . . .

You get to the last house, and it's perfect. There's a decent-sized front lawn, and a secluded garden at the back. The roof is only a month old, and the plumbing has just been upgraded. What do you think? The Good.

Recruiters use exactly the same method to place job-seekers. But they send candidates out on interviews to companies instead of taking the company out to look at horrible houses. The next time you go to an interview arranged by a recruiter, ask yourself, 'Am I the Good, the Bad, or the Ugly'?

It's certainly a dirty trick, but it isn't the dirtiest one I've heard of. Over the years a few clients have told me about a situation where they were discreetly putting their CV on the job websites (don't snigger) and were approached by a recruiter. Within a few days they were called into their boss's office and confronted by the fact that they were looking for work and, if that was the case, they were now free to look full-time.

It seems that one of the nastiest tricks in the recruiters' repertoire is to find a candidate, sign him up, and then go to his manager, saying that he understands so-and-so is looking for work, so he'll soon be needing to fill the vacancy. The recruiter then tells your manager that he has several great candidates, and would he be interested in meeting them? It kills two birds with one stone. He now has you safely in his database, and he has a company that is now aggressively looking to fill a newly vacant job role!

How Many Jobs Did You Lose Out On Because Of That Huge Price Tag Hovering Over Your Head?

How many times have you gone to interviews arranged by recruiters, knowing you were the best candidate? You even knew that your salary requirements were in line with their budget and, yet, it ends with the company recruiting internally or, suddenly, finding a 'more closely matched candidate'. Why do you think that happened? Is it because you have a third eye growing from your forehead that you can't see when you look in the mirror? Is it because you aren't as talented and successful as you'd like to think you are? NO. It's because you were much more expensive than you realised.

I talk to people every day who tell me they aren't interested in using my company's services because they aren't going to pay to look for work. They will, instead, use a recruiter because they get their fee paid by the company. Yes, the company pays the recruiter's fees, but that money comes straight out of your pocket!

When a company agrees to take on a candidate represented by a recruiter, it is agreeing to spend a proportion of their overall recruitment budget to do so. That means that they have to offer the candidate less start-up money. It doesn't end there.

If the manager has a budget of, let's say, £70,000 to recruit a person for a job, with the recruitment consultant charging a very conservative 15% commission, £10,500 automatically goes to the recruiter! So, putting you into the equation, a manager has a budget of £70,000, but he has to build in the recruiter's fee, which means that the most he can offer you is £59,500. Year one, and you've already had a 15% pay cut! The next year comes along and it's time for pay rises! When you sit down with your boss, he does your evaluation and determines that you have been doing a great job, and he is going to give you a 5% performance increase, plus a 3% cost-of-living raise. Of course, these increases are all based on your (already-too-low) starting salary of £59,500, so your 8% rise now gives you only £4,760! In one year's time you have already spent a grand total of £16,100 in hard-earned, but-never-seen, money!

If you were a manager and you understood your budget and your options, and you had six other candidates to choose from without a big price tag on their heads, would you pay the recruiter?

How Does It Feel To Be A CV In A Database?

Recruiters are just as inundated with CVs as most large companies. I've spoken to recruiters who tell me it's not uncommon for them to receive a thousand or more emailed CVs in a day, and sometimes another hundred or more paper CVs on a good day! They are forced to use the same software programs that HR departments use, just to categorise all the CVs they receive. The job-seeker quickly becomes human chattel, reduced to a database, being managed on a wholesale basis. When a recruiter gets your CV, he wants to be able to quickly sort you into the appropriate file. That means that later on, when he finds a company willing to accept applicants from him, he can reach into the right file, grab a handful of people who match their requirements, and quickly pass them on to the company! Your individual skills, needs and wants don't really enter into the equation. When he calls you about an opportunity, he's not trying to discern your needs and desires; he's just trying to get you interested. He wants to hear you agree to his commission so that he can add you to the pile of people he's putting in front of that company. Recruiters don't have the time to think of job-seekers as individuals. Instead, they think of quotas, goals, commissions and how many candidates they can add to their collection so that, when the chance to sell someone comes along, they have the best odds of closing the deal with one of their products.

Why They Don't Care If It's You Or Bob Who Gets The Job (As Long As It's One Of Theirs)

The thing to understand about recruiters is that they're not working for you. Each one is working for himself. His goal is not the altruistic desire to see you get a job that makes you happy and fulfils your needs. His goal is to place a candidate this month in order to cover his overheads, pay the mortgage, and feed his family.

The way he does this is by getting as many of his dogs into the fight as he can. If that recruiter has one player in the game, his chances of success aren't all that good, but if he can get 10 of his players in there, working hard to beat each other in their desperate attempt to get that job, the recruiter has just improved his odds tenfold. He's rooting for you to win. He's rooting for the other candidates to win. He really wants one of you to win, because as long as it's one of his players, he's the winner.

He's on your side and he's working for you – but only in the sense that if you win the lottery, he's already got his hooks into you and you have to share the winnings. It's the same for most of the other candidates who are trying to get the job: He's on their side, as well, hoping that they get the job, too.

13. Why You Are Unemployed or Still in the Same Old Job

I talk to people all the time who have been actively looking for work for six months, a year, even two years! They aren't that bad at their real job! If you had spent six months or a year with no results at your last job, it's very likely you would be fired for your poor performance. You would be amazed how many otherwise completely successful people are out of work for what seems to be a very long time. If I found myself out of work for more than a few weeks, I would start to seriously question my abilities and value as a human being – and I know these people question themselves, too. They aren't bad people or unworthy of being employed. They're just not very good at looking for work.

'If you performed as badly on the job as you did looking for the job, you'd be fired!'

When I talk to someone who has been actively looking for work (as opposed to those people who have been actively working on procrastinating for the last six months) for many months, sometimes more than a year, and the two things they have in common are an underlying sense of desperation and depression, and the unfailing opinion that it's the economy and their specialised industry that's causing their job search to go on so long.

I understand the depression (I would be depressed, too), but I totally disagree on the second point. If you've spent more than 10 minutes in the workforce, you have accumulated enough skills and experience to break out of your field and into something else if your industry or specialisation is dying. The real reason these individuals spend such great lengths of time looking for work is because they aren't very good at it and they are out of touch with what is really going on around them.

Human Resources: The Black Hole Of Death!

One of the main reasons your job search is taking so long is because you are sending your CV to the last place it needs to go, instead of the first place it should go! Why did you send your CV to HR? Was it an accident? Did you mean to address it to someone who would have a clue about what you do and how it could benefit the company, or were you just under the false impression that HR recruits people?

An HR employee's real purpose

A human resource employee's only real duty when it comes to recruiting other employees is to manage posted job advertisements. HR drones don't actually do the recruiting; they're just charged with filtering out the wheat from the chaff. They work from a set list of requirements needed for a specific position to be filled. If there isn't a clear description for a position, HR drones are entirely ill-equipped to handle unsolicited CVs. If they don't have an order for a position, they are completely unable to work out what to do with a CV, so their knee-jerk reaction is to file it away.

HR has no command in a company's chain of command

A big company is a dictatorship, not a democracy. The CEO is the captain, and there is a very rigid chain of command that trickles down from there. If you were to look at that chain, you wouldn't only find HR at the end of the chain. It would be on a separate chain altogether!

The main duties of HR departments are to deal with the policies and procedures affecting existing employees and those related to employment regulations, such as equal opportunities. In reality, an HR department is simply a company's administrative arm concerned with internal issues affecting employees already working for the company. They aren't there to do the recruitment, and they definitely don't have the authority to employ anyone over entry-level.

'HR has never recruited anyone above entry-level.'

Stop! Before you send me an email to tell me that you were recruited by the HR director, stop and think this through. I recently spoke to a client of mine who is Director of Operations for a medium sized packaging company. During the course of my conversation, I commented that HR had never recruited someone at his level. He stopped me and proceeded to tell me that he had actually been recruited by the HR director at his last job. He then went on to explain that when he sent his CV to the CEO of the company, the CEO called the HR department and told them to give my client a call, and that, if he was as impressive in person as he was on paper, to employ him on the spot! That HR drone didn't act on his own. That's not his job. He followed the instructions of the CEO.

An interview with an HR drone: An exposé on your CV's journey into the black hole

The following story is completely true. Only the names, places, and events have been changed to protect the guilty. An anonymous human resources employee, Jayne Claremont, who works for a large unidentified company, National Widget Products, recently confided the following events.

Last month, Jim, the Assistant Manager of Product Development, came to her because he had been fruitlessly searching for a new star that could turn a failing site around. Jim had been searching within the company for several months with no luck, and it was now time to reach out to the rest of the world before the factory completely failed. His biggest hurdle was that he couldn't define what he needed. He'd become completely frustrated and, as a measure of his desperation, he had gone to the HR department to pass the search onto them. 'No problem,' Jayne said. 'That's what we're here for.'

'So, what are you looking for?' she asks him.

'I haven't a clue; that's why I'm here,' Jim replies.

Jayne stares at him. Is he joking? 'You've got to give us a list of candidate requirements and a list of key words for the filters.'

'Filters?'

'Filters? Yes, filters. We'll be getting hundreds of CVs every day.
There's no way we can look at all of them, so we'll just use the
"robot" to filter them,' she says, 'So. What do you want us to
look for?'

'Eh?' Jim is starting to get that annoying headache again.

'You know, education, years of experience, specific software
expertise, unique abilities, length of time in the industry –
those things.'

'I'm looking for someone to turnaround the factory before it
goes under!'

'Oh, "turnaround". What else? How about education?' 'I don't
know! I suppose I need a graduate, if he's going to save
the site . . .'

'OK, graduate. Now we're getting somewhere!' Jayne is
excited now.

Outplacement And Severance

Quite often I talk to people who have been looking for work for
several months, and they're really discouraged about their prospects
because they have been getting help all along the way. Or so they
thought. Again and again I talk to people who tell me they are already
getting the services that my company offers because their last employer
provided them with outplacement. Nothing could be further from the
truth. When you understand how outplacement works, and why, you'll
quickly realise that you are grabbing on to lead weights in the hope of
keeping yourself afloat.

The unconscionable business model of outplacement

The very way outplacement works makes it a lost cause when it comes
to finding work. Outplacement is paid for by your former employer,
based on the number of weeks that you use their service. If you got
paid hundreds of pounds for every week that a person came into your
office and sat in one of your 'executive cubicles', using your phones
and using your photocopier, would you be motivated to get them out
of your place quickly? Not likely!

That's why you spend several days in 'CV-writing' seminars, followed by several days of personality testing and video analyses, and being given information on companies, one at a time. Their goal is to drag the re-employment process out for as long as possible. One of the main reasons (motivation) your past employer has for paying your outplacement is to give you a 'cooling off' period. They want to keep you off the market as long as possible. They let go of someone who has a considerable knowledge of their business and competition, and sent him back into the working world. The last thing they want to see is you getting a job with one of their competitors. So, what better way to prevent this happening than to send you to an adult childcare centre that understands their role: To keep you off the market as long as possible. If you've been in outplacement, how long were you there before they started the spiel about 'starting your own business'? If you're in outplacement right now, ask your careers advisers how many of them got their job after being placed in the very same scheme by their last employer? I think you'd be very surprised at the percentage!

Avoiding wrongful dismissal cases and drunken ex-employees 'going postal'

When a company lets go of an employee, or even hundreds of employees at once, they run the risk of being hit by wrongful dismissal lawsuits. What better way to deal with that during the trial than to say, 'Your honour, we even went as far as providing him with outplacement! We felt truly bad about letting him go, so we did everything we could to get him back to work as fast as possible. It's not our fault that he was unemployable.'

The other concern they have is that disgruntled ex-employees will turn up at the workplace. By sending the employee to an outplacement company, they provide that newly displaced worker with a place to express their frustrations and trained advisers who understand that it is their job to keep that disgruntled employee preoccupied with starting their own fruit-smoothie franchise.

Severance: the recipe for a ruined career

Another trick is to provide you with severance. Companies do this as another way to stop you suing them. After all, how can they be the baddie when they carried on paying you your salary long after you left?

They know it's very likely that you won't look for work during the severance period. Yes, you tell yourself you are looking for work while you're receiving that severance payment, but just how motivated are you? You've worked hard your whole working life, so what's wrong with taking a little hard-earned 'me time'? Perhaps I'll just relax for a few days before I get back to the job search. After all, I'm a great catch, I've never even had to look for work before. They've always come to me! Finding another job shouldn't take more than a few days, a month at the very most, and I've got 12 months of severance! I could take the whole summer off and still be back to work before it runs out . . .

Double-dipping: it is OK

Double-dipping on a severance payment should be your number one goal! To people who feel that it is wrong, or immoral, or bad etiquette to take a new job and continue receiving severance pay, think again! You got fired by that company. They knew they were treating you badly, and they were willing to pay you off to keep you from coming back at them. It's your money. You earned it, and they agreed to give it to you. Now it's your duty to go out there and find a new job. Don't think that waiting until your severance runs out won't affect your chances of getting another job. The longer you're off the market, the less desirable you become to another employer. Take a full year off to enjoy your severance pay, and you'll end up as the least attractive candidate in the running.

The 12-Month Plan For Reemployment

Don't take the serial approach

The top reason so many people spend an enormous amount of time on their job search is because they approach it in a serial fashion.

(I'm not referring to the fact that they spend more than half the day sitting around the house in their underwear eating cereal instead of working aggressively to find a job.) They pursue opportunities one at a time. On Monday, Sally from the HR department at National Widget calls about a vacancy in their design department. You have a great phone interview and end the call by scheduling a face-to-face interview on Wednesday. Excellent! You've got this job search thing in the bag! You've done so well on Monday that you take the rest of the day off, and on Tuesday you don't really feel like you've got to make too much of an effort, seeing as you've practically been offered a job at National Widget. Wednesday comes, you go to the interview, it goes well, and they tell you they will let you know in a few days. A few days go by and you start to get the 'the manager is on holiday' routine. Within a week you start to realise that this isn't panning out, so it's back to the grindstone. Two weeks of job searching are lost.

The irons-in-the-fire method for long-term job searching

Another mistaken approach is the 'I've got quite a few irons in the fire' mind game. Usually this means that you have had calls from several companies, and they've promised to get back with you by the end of blah blah blah. The more irons you stick in the fire, the more complacent you become in your job search. Before you know it, you've become so consumed with tracking down those irons, and they've got so cold from sitting in a dying fire, that your job search dwindles off to a smouldering ruin.

An iron in the fire is a job offer in hand. Anything short of that is just a wish and a prayer. If you don't spend the greater part of your energy fanning the flames, your irons will never get red-hot. Activity isn't the end result (unlike the popular belief of my clients, who felt that they were being very successful in their job search because they were getting a steady stream of emails from job website postings). The end goal is to have multiple job offers in hand. Until you reach that goal, slowing down is not an option.

Redecorating the bathroom, the kitchen, the living room...

A perfect recipe for disaster is letting your significant other give you a list of DIY jobs to do while you're unemployed and looking for work. If you find yourself in a situation where you have been given a list of home improvements to take care of while you are looking for a job, *stop*.

The first thing you need to do is sit down with your partner and explain that right now is one of the most critical times in your whole career. The actions you take now will seriously affect both of your lives. Your only job at this time is to look for work. By asking you to regrout the bathroom tiles or repaint the kitchen, he or she is using an unskilled worker at the wage of a highly skilled professional. Your family is not only agreeing to pay you your hourly wage in lost income; they are agreeing to spend money at a time when there is less, or even NO MONEY, coming into the household.

If you earn £55,000 a year, and you end up working on projects around the house for just two weeks (and once you get started on those DIY projects, the weeks will fly by), you have just spent around £2,200 to mend a leaking toilet, repaint the back room or clean out the loft! And, because that was 'lost wages' money, you're actually spending twice as much, because you spent that money when you didn't have money coming in to pay for the mortgage, the groceries, the cost of your kids . . . If you and your family can afford to spend money that extravagantly, you don't need to look for work, because you're rich!

Interview Errors You Don't Know You're Making

Grilling the interviewer

So many people think that they are doing brilliantly at an interview because they ask lots of probing questions about the company, the role and the other employees. They mistakenly behave as if they're Jeremy Paxman on *Newsnight*. What they don't realise is that they're doing nothing to sell themselves and are actually putting the interviewer on the defensive or, at best, completely distracting him from your goal, which is to impress him with what makes you a great candidate.

How could asking the interviewer what the company's product lines are and how much they sell in a year, possibly get across how impressive a salesman you are? Asking that interviewer how much an average salesman earns in commissions says to him, 'I'm not really keen on your company or your products, and I'm trying to determine if I could survive, if I came to work for you'. Does that message convey that you are an above average salesperson, one who is confident and eager to prove himself, if given the chance? Not at all. As I've said before, if you aren't saying something that definitely sells you as the best candidate for the job, you are saying something that is damaging your chances of getting the job. Save the questions about the company and the products for after they have made an offer.

Avoiding the questions

You think you've dodged a bullet by babbling a load of small talk but, in reality, the only one impressed with it is you. An interviewer sees through you and is not impressed with the candidate who isn't prepared and can't answer the tough questions. Being prepared is the number one way to overcome this problem. Do your homework before you show up. Write down all the questions you're most afraid of tackling and write out an answer for each. Keep doing this until you can't think of another question. Now, go in there and be prepared to be caught out! They'll always find a way to trip you up. That's OK. Just have a good response to as many as you can, and if they hit you with something you've never considered before, sometimes the best approach is to tell the interviewer that you have never considered that before, and that you are quite impressed with his question! (Throwing a complimentary smokescreen at the interviewer is always a good start to a bad situation. Everyone likes praise.)

I think on my feet

Thinking you're a great communicator and can speak spontaneously on any given subject is a great way to ruin an interview. Preparation is the key to success. If you don't have an outline of what you want to achieve in the interview, then you're relying on the interviewer to steer the meeting. That interviewer has no motivation to try to help you in an interview; his or her goal is to quickly ferret out the riffraff and wait to be wowed by the quality candidates. If you don't have a plan to do that, you are just waiting for a chance to say the wrong thing.

Did I put that on my CV?

Always, always bring a copy of your CV with you to an interview, and always have one near the phone. Be completely in the know about everything you've put in your CV, and DON'T LIE ABOUT ANYTHING!

The best way to discredit yourself is to contradict yourself by saying something that conflicts with what's on your CV. You have an incredible outline of your career and achievements in your CV! Use it that way, and you won't be one of the many clients I've worked with who have painted themselves into a corner and had to confess what they really meant to say.

14. The Fears, Phobias and Fallacies Holding You Back

(And How to Overcome Them)

Looking for work is tough. It's scary, it's a lot of hard work, it's full of rejection and criticism, and there are people who don't know half as much as you about the job, telling you that you aren't right for the job! It's also tough because everyone tells you something different about what you should do to find work.

It's very challenging. Trust me, I know. I've done it many times in the past, and I hated every minute of it, every time. I'm sure I'll have to look for work again before I die, and I'm sure I won't love doing it. But at least I know that I will be successful and that ultimately I will find another great job that makes me happy, and keeps food on the table and the debt collectors off my back.

As the great Franklin D. Roosevelt once said, 'The only thing we have to fear, is fear itself'. Of course, when you really think about it, if you fear fear itself you're still afraid, which remains an issue to be dealt with! I'm sure that when he said that he was just hoping the emotion of the moment would get everyone excited and that they would completely overlook that little loophole in his logic. The point he was really trying to make is that things seem scary only when you don't understand them.

Now you understand what you're up against, and you know how to use those things to your advantage. There's nothing scary about answering a few simple questions about yourself. Printing your CV and addressing it to people you've never met at a company you've never heard of isn't a life-or-death thing. You know what to expect in the interviews, and you already have the answers to their questions in front of you. The pressure is off when it comes to crafting the perfect email response to a posting on a job website.

You now know that you can use the same response for all of them, get it done in the first few minutes of your day, and go on with your life. Recruiters have lost their mystical aura, you've seen behind the curtain, and just as the Wizard of Oz said, 'There's nothing to see here.' Don't let your fear and your misplaced beliefs get in the way of your success. Everything you've read in this book was learned by actually doing it.

Are You Participating In 'Notworks'?

One of the worst things I hear from my clients is that they have joined networking groups with other unemployed people. I call them 'not working networks' or 'notworks'. Can you imagine thinking that you're going to be more successful in your job search by surrounding yourself with other unemployed people? Think about it. All these people are competing with you for a job. If they come across a good opportunity, what's their motivation to tell you about it? The only people likely to share their newfound opportunities with you are the truly foolish ones and so it's very possible that the opportunities they unearth won't be the cream of the crop.

Aside from well meaning, but misguided 'notwork' contacts, your wife, husband, friend, mentor or family may also want to help. You should ask yourself: does this person really know anything about looking for work? Have they been conducting job searches every day for years? The answer is very likely to be no. Nod your head, thank them for their advice and walk away! They all want to help in one way or another (always be aware of the other person's motives), but it's more than likely they can't help you as much as they would like. The key to success is finding someone who is already successful and doing what they do.

Success Is Easier Than You Think: Work Smarter, Not Harder!

It's a fact. Looking for a job is hard work, but that doesn't mean you can't do it. You now have a game plan or road map to get where you want to be! Follow the steps, put your heart into the work, and, before you know it, you will be starting that new job, getting a great salary and loving life again. This method has helped thousands of people find great jobs and it will do it for you too, as long as you go out there and DO IT!

Conclusion

Wrapping It Up

Now you understand what you've been doing wrong in your job search and what you *should* be doing to be successful. It's now time to stop reading and start *doing*.

As I tell my clients all the time: You can have the greatest CV in the world but, if you don't get it out in front of the right people (and enough of them), you might as well stick that CV in a desk drawer and forget it. (Conversely, you could have a truly poor CV, but if you get it in front of the right people, often enough, you will, eventually, get results.) The key is exposure.

You have the tools to create a great CV that will show the reader who you are, what you've done, and how you could help them. You also know how to write a winning covering letter that quickly tells the reader why you are approaching them, what you have done in the past that proves you're successful, and compels them to want to learn more about you.

You know the secrets to getting great exposure. Find companies that need someone like you and find the right person in that company to get in front of, the recruiting decision-maker, not the human resources drones! You now understand the power of a great CV, and of the other methods for getting your name out there: recruiters, job websites, your network, the 'Holy Trinity'. You know that everything in moderation is good, but that nothing in the extreme can be healthy.

You know how to make a good impression in the interview and someone has, finally, told you to stop making all those foolish beginner's mistakes! You have the ability to hold your own in the salary negotiations, and you know when and how to ask for that big, juicy sign-on bonus. You have everything you need to go out there and start generating multiple job offers and find the dream job that you deserve. The last step in the process is for you now is to get up and DO IT!

Further Information

SIC listings

Office for National Statistics (National Statistics Online)
The Office for National Statistics website gives full information about
UK SIC codes and gives the full list of codes.
www.statistics.gov.uk/sic

UK business databases

Dun & Bradstreet Key British Enterprises
https://solutions.dnb.com/kbe/

Bureau Van Dyke's FAME
https://fame.bvdep.com/cgi/template.dll?product=1

Other resources for list information:

Links to regional chambers of commerce websites
www.britishchambers.org.uk/

Business Link – information and links to regional centres
www.businesslink.gov.uk

**Companies House – information on UK business registered with
companies house**
www.companieshouse.gov.uk

National *Yellow Pages* with company information
www.yell.com

Thomson Directories, Business Strata
www.thomsondirectories.com/directmarketing.aspx

Salary information

Worksmart
www.worksmart.org.uk/tools/pay.php

Prospects
www.prospects.ac.uk

Index

A

answering machine, 60
appointments, book, 86
attitude, poor, 79

B

bullet points, using, 126

C

career path, is job offer
    in line with, 91
challenges, does your work
    provide you with enough, 130
cold-calling, 58
colour logos, 48
commitments, get all in writing,
    102–103
communications, human,
    17–18
company hierarchy, understand
    your place in, 40
contacts, networking new,
    57–58
counteroffers, making, 89–93
covering letter as tag-team
    salesmen, CV and, 15–16
    as agent for CV, 19
    date on your, 51
    writing your, 27–29
creative side,
    listening to your, 13

CV and covering letter as
    tag-team salesmen, 15–16,
    18–19
CV reader, know your, 119–120
    colleagues as, 120–121
    friends and family as, 120
    recruiters as, 121
CV scanners, 137–138
CV, achievement-based, 123
    buzzword, 123–124
    company director as first job,
        122–123
    faxing, 128
    gaps in, 125–126
    getting it to the right people,
        39, 40–41, 45–46
    one page to two page,
        124–125
    picture on your, 48, 126–127
    style of, 119, 121–125, 126
    the six-pack, 19–22

D

dates of employment on CV,
    23–24
Day 1 Assignment – Step 1, 11–12
    Step 2, 12–13
    Step 3, 13–14
Day 2 Assignment – Step 1,
    24–26
    Step 2, 26–27
    Step 3, 27–29

Day 3 Assignment – Step 1, 40
  Step 2, 40–41
  Step 3, 41–43
Days 4 and 5 Assignment –
  Step 1, 53
  Step 2, 53
  Step 3, 53
Day 6 Assignment – Step 1,
  61
  Step 2, 61–62
  Step 3, 62
Days 7, 8, and 9 Assignment –
  Step 1, 86
  Step 2, 86
  Step 3, 86
Day 10 Assignment – Step 1, 92
  Step 2, 92
  Step 3, 92–93
dial-up connection for internet,
  60
direct mail,
  depressing realities of, 55–57
direct mail marketing, 31–32
direct mail rejection, 56
direct marketing, 3
do-it-yourself marketing,
  dos and don'ts, 46–53
Dun & Bradstreet, 56, 165

E

envelopes, 49–50
  addressing, 49–50
expectations correctly, set your,
  84–85

F

face-to-face interview, 7 deadlier
  sins of the, 77–81
follow up with every
  opportunity, 59, 62
format dos and don'ts, 22–24

G

Good, the Bad, and the Ugly
  game, the, 144–146
Google, 42

H

'Hidden Job Market,' 1
hobbies on CV, 24
'Holy Trinity' of job search,
  the, 5
  the truth about the,
    133–134
HR drone,
  interview with an,
    151–152
HR employee,
  real purpose of, 150–151

I

industry, evaluate your, 129–130
inkjet printer, 48–49
internet, the, 42
interview,
  accept every, 77
  basic dos and don'ts, 79–81
  mistakes, 156–158

never leave without knowing where you stand in an, 81–82

interview questions, avoiding, 157

interviewer, grilling the, 156–157

interviews, multiple, 59

J

job, key elements that will make a great, 92

job offer, accepting more than one, 87–90

job offers, evaluate, 92–93
    game plan for collecting, 92

job search as full-time work, 2
    exposure as key to successful, 31, 46, 163
    ongoing, 109–110, 111
    professional attitude about, 60–61

job search marketing plan, three basic ingredients of, 117–118

job-seekers, passive, 134, 136

job websites, 5, 112, 133
    as part of 'Holy Trinity,' 133–137
    postings on, 136–137

K

KISS principle, 19, 22
    with covering letter, 27–28

L

laser printer, 49

letter, undelivered, 55, 56

leverage in negotiating jobs, 88–90

list, format for your, 42
    links for, 43–44
    marketing, 32–34

list provider, work with a, 41–42

lists, alternate sources for, 42–44
    chamber of commerce, 42–43

libraries, 43

M

mail merge, 49

mailing list companies 34, 36–42

mailing, timing your, 50–51

marketing plan, developing your, 32–36

market value, maximum, 59

marketing materials, your, 119–122

marketing, dos and don'ts of do-it-yourself, 46–53

MS Office mail merge, 49

N

name on CV, 22–23

negotiate,
    three Cs to consider before you, 105–108
    company conditions, 107
    industry conditions, 106–107
    your condition, 107–108

negotiating for a better salary,
excuses for not, 95–97
*Negotiating Your Salary: How to
Make $1000 a Minute*, 104
network,
maintain your real, 113
mining your, 43
who is your real, 142
your, 5–6
networking, 133–136
as part of 'Holy Trinity,'
127–128
new contacts, 57–58
non-compete agreement,
113–115
'notworking networks' 160
numbers game, the, 103–104

O

objective on CV, 23
offers, keep on the table,
110–111
office supply stores, 48, 51–52
Open Office, 49
opportunity as special, treat
every, 75–76, 77–78
outplacement, business model of,
152–153

P

paper, choosing covering letter
and envelope, 47–48
choosing CV, 46–47
past employment, keep records
of, 25–26

pay rise, have you asked your
current employer for a, 131
personal data on CV, 24
phone interview, first, 75–76
7 deadly sins of the, 77–78
position build-up, creating a,
19–20
six questions in each, 24–26
sample, 27
price tag, your huge, 146–147
print shops, 51–52, 53
printing services, professional, 48
printing, choosing means for,
48–49
professional help with mailing,
51–52
promotion, have you asked for a,
131–132

R

recruiters/recruitment
consultants, 5–6, 33, 112–113,
119, 120, 124, 127, 133, 135
as part of 'Holy Trinity,'
142–148
difference between retained
and contingent, 143–144
dirty tricks of, 144–148
reemployment, 12-month plan
for, 154–156
irons in the fire method, 155
references on CV, 24
relocation reimbursement, 101–
102
results, quantifiable, 22

S

salary expectations and market value, 97–99

salary figure, know your minimum, 103

salary negotiating and fear, 96–97
and skill level, 96
and the economy, 95
and the industry, 95–96
and worth, 96

salary requirements in covering letter, 100–101

sales plan, components of a solid, 118

second choice, never make a company think that they're your, 82–84

self-analysis, conduct a, 129–130

selling yourself, practice, 76, 86

severance, 154

SIC codes, 34–35
history of, 35–36

SIC codes for your industries, look up, 38

SIC codes, links for, 43–44

sign-on bonus, getting a, 101–103
warnings about, 103

skills, define your transferable, 12
situation-oriented, 9–11
transferable, 9

spamming your next employer, don't, 127

stamps, 53

Standard Industrial Classification. see SIC codes

story of your career, tell, 17–18

summary section, one-size-fits-all, 125

'sweat equity' in direct marketing, how much, 51, 53, 58

T

tag-team salesmen, CV and covering letter as, 15–16, 19

targets, first-level, 14
second-level, 14

TBNT ('Thanks, But No Thanks') pile, 16
letters, 56

10-Day Method, the, 7

thank-you letters, 57
sample, 63–73

U

understanding your market, 9–11

V

voicemail, 60

W

Who Moved My Cheese?, 130

win-win situation, 108

work, actively looking for, 149
looking for, 159–161

worth, determining your, 98–99

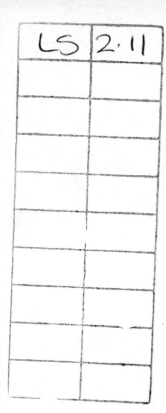

LS	2.11